MAMME DEAR

MAMME DEAR

A Turn-of-the-Century Collection of Model Yiddish Letters

translated and with an introduction by Lewis Glinert

JASON ARONSON INC.
Northvale, New Jersey
Jerusalem

This book was set in 12 pt. Tiffany by Alabama Book Composition of Deatsville, Alabama.

Copyright © 1997 by Lewis Glinert

10 9 8 7 6 5 4 3 2 1

All rights reserved. Printed in the United States of America. No part of this book may be used or reproduced in any manner whatsoever without written permission from Jason Aronson Inc. except in the case of brief quotations in reviews for inclusion in a magazine, newspaper, or broadcast.

The author gratefully acknowledges Hebrew Publishing Company at P.O. Box 157, Rockaway Beach, NY 11693, for their permission to reprint the Yiddish text.

Library of Congress Cataloging-in-Publication Data

Blaustein's brivenshteler. English. Selections.
   Mamme dear : a turn-of-the-century collection of model Yiddish letters / translated with an introduction and notes by Lewis Glinert.
      p.   cm.
   Translation of 112 model letters from Blaustein's brivenshteler.
   Includes bibliographical references.
   ISBN 0-7657-5982-9 (alk. paper)
   1. Letter writing, Yiddish. 2. Yiddish letters—Translations into English. I. Glinert, Lewis. II. Title.
PJ5118.B56132 1997
839'.16308—dc21   96-45382

Manufactured in the United States of America. Jason Aronson Inc. offers books and cassettes. For information and catalog write to Jason Aronson Inc., 230 Livingston Street, Northvale, New Jersey 07647.

For my *shviger,*
isho tovas sechel
Blanche Berman-Abraham

Contents

Acknowledgements   xii

Introduction   1

FAMILY LETTERS   37

  1   A Father to a Son   37
  2   Reply   39

  3   A Son to a Father   40

  4   Parents to a Son   41

  5   A Daughter to a Mother   43
  6   Reply   45

  7   A Brother to a Sister   47
  8   Reply   49

  9   A Sister to a Brother   51
10   Reply   53

11   A Mother to a Son   55
12   Reply   57

13   A Mother to a Daughter   59
14   Reply   61

15	A Father to a Son	63
16	Reply	65
17	One Brother to Another	67
18	Reply	69
19	Wolf to Solomon	71
20	Solomon to Wolf	73
21	Wolf to Solomon	75
22	Solomon to Wolf	77
23	One Brother to Another	79
24	Reply	80
25	Shimon to Boruch	82
26	Reply	83
27	Shimon to Boruch	85
28	A Nephew to an Uncle	86
29	One Sister to Another	87
30	Reply	89
31	Rose to Lina	90
32	Lina to Rose	92
33	A Sister to a Brother	93
34	Reply	94
35	Max to Yitzchok	95
36	Reply	96

LOVE LETTERS — 97

37	Phillip to Anna	97
38	Anna to Phillip	99
39	Phillip to Anna	101
40	Anna to Phillip	103

41	Phillip to Anna	104
42	Anna to Phillip	106

LETTERS BETWEEN FIANCÉS 109

43	To One's Fiancée	109
44	Reply	111
45	Shimon to Naomi	112
46	Naomi to Shimon	114
47	To One's Fiancée	115
48	Reply	117
49	To One's Fiancé	118
50	From an Ex-Fiancée	120
51	Reply	122

LETTERS BETWEEN HUSBAND AND WIFE 123

52	A Husband to a Wife	123
53	Reply	125
54	A Wife to a Husband	127
55	Reply	129
56	A Husband to a Wife	131
57	Reply	133
58	A Wife to a Husband	135
59	Reply	137
60	A Husband to a Wife	139
61	In Another Manner	140
62	A Wife to Her Husband	141
63	Reply	143
64	Rosa to Isaac	145

65	A Husband to His Wife	147
66	Reply	149
67	Pinchas to Perl	151
68	Chaim to Nechome	153
69	Nechome to Chaim	154
70	A Wife to a Husband	155
71	Reply	156
72	A Wife to a Husband	158

LETTERS TO FRIENDS 159

73	To a Woman Friend	159
74	Reply	161
75	Tanya to Klara	163
76	To a Woman Friend	164
77	To a Male Friend	165
78	Reply	167
79	To a Male Friend	169
80	Reply	171
81	Michael to Raphael	173
82	To a Male Friend	175
83	Reply	177
84	Benjamin to Bunem	178
85	Bunem to Benjamin	180
86	Benjamin to Bunem	181

MAKING A MATCH 183

87	To a Matchmaker	183
88	Reply	185

89	A Matchmaker to an In-law	186
90	Reply	188
91	To a Matchmaker	190
92	Reply	192

LETTERS TO INQUIRY (FOR *SHIDUKHIM*) 193

93	Chaim to Shimon	193
94	Shimon to Chaim	195
95	In Another Manner	196
96	In Another Manner	197

LETTERS OF INVITATION 199

97	To a Wedding	199
98	Reply	201
99	To an Engagement	202
100	To a Bris	203

LETTER OF CONGRATULATION 205

101	Letter to a Friend	205

LETTER OF CONDOLENCE 207

102	On the Death of a Friend's Wife	207

LETTERS FROM CHILDREN 209

103	From a Child to Parents	209
104	To a Brother	210
105	To a Sister	211
106	To an Uncle	212

107	To a Grandfather	213
108	To a Good Friend	214
109	Reply	215
110	A Boy to His Friend	216
111	To a Friend	217
112	A Pupil to a Teacher	218

Acknowledgements

I am grateful to Joseph Bar-El, Thomas Beebee, Joshua Fishman and Dovid Katz for their advice and assistance with this book. I also wish to thank Mr. Charles Lieber of The Hebrew Publishing Company, publishers of *Steinberg's Brivenshteler*.

Introduction

Few genres of Yiddish literature have gone so unacknowledged as the Yiddish letter-writing manual, the *Brivenshteler*. It is not, on the face of it, a form of literature at all, but a collection of letters demonstrating how to express oneself, maybe how to behave, and how to view the world. In this sense, it was awarded a high profile by the great ethnographers of the *shtetl*, Zborowski and Herzog:[1]

"And among the best sellers of all is the *brifshteller*, the 'letter-composer,' with model letters to fit any occasion. Hundreds of women in hundreds of towns will write to their husbands identical letters, copied out of some *brifshteller*, each telling her man about her special affection and esteem for him and about the health of their children."[2]

---

1. Mark Zborowski and Elizabeth Herzog, *Life is with People* (New York: International Universities Press, 1952), p. 127.
2. Of course, countless women could not even read a *Brivenshteler*, like Sheindel in I. J. Singer's *East of Eden*

And in this sense, clearly, the *Brivenshteler* partakes of a long and illustrious tradition of letter-writing manuals across Europe. However, as is abundantly clear from the history of the Western novel, letter-writing manuals also eventually tended to create a narrative or set of narratives in their own right, an epistolary fiction—and from this sprang Samuel Richardson's *Pamela* (1741) and Rousseau's *La Nouvelle Héloïse* (1761), firstfruits of the classic European novel.

In its two hundred years of recorded history,[3] the Yiddish *Brivenshteler*, too, has come to tell a narrative and to serve humble creative ends. Particularly when viewed systematically in the context of Yiddish literature as a whole in the late nineteenth century, when the short story and the novel were in their infancy, the humble letter-writing manual with its covert dramas and lyrical outbursts occupied its own significant place in the menu of what was essentially a folk literature.[4] The full extent of its influence is yet to be gauged.

Not that any and every letter-writing manual of

(New York: Alfred Knopf Inc., 1939), p. 88: "If she were only able to, she would write to her father; the only alternative to writing oneself is to go to a professional letter-writer."

3. The fullest treatment to date is Joseph Bar-El's *The Yiddish Briefenshteler (letter writing manual) of the 18th to the 20th century*, Ph.D. dissertation, 1970.

4. Popular satirical and sentimental novels and short stories were all the rage. The first truly best sellers were Linetzky's satire *Dos Poilishe Yingl* (1867) and Dineson's *Der Shvartser Yingermantshik* (1877), the latter selling 200,000 copies (Sol Liptzin, *The Flowering of Yiddish Literature*, New York: Yoseloff, 1963).

the day had these qualities. Thus, the *English Letter-Writer*[5], edited by Alexander Harkavy for Jewish immigrants to the United States, is devoted almost entirely to commercial letters, job applications, complaints to landlords, and the like.

In offering the first English edition of a modern Yiddish *Brivenshteler*, it is with a touch of irony that I have chosen *Blaustein's Brivenshteler*, or, as it was to become known to a generation of American Jews, *Steinberg's Brivenshteler*. Written not by an eminent Yiddishist and lexicographer like Alexander Harkavy but by an unknown hand—the author is referred to solely by the initials *ches-shin-nun*—this letter-writing manual from the turn-of-the-century has few literary or social pretensions, yet the hundred-odd letters are a kaleidoscopic reflection of Jewish life at the time of the mass migrations, a hubbub of voices and views from both the Old and the New World, at times intriguing or disturbing and at times just touching. That these are not the actual voices but imagined ones is, in one way, just part of the literary game. The anonymous author or authors have left us with a set of narratives that may not portray anything approaching individual characters whom we can explore and with whom we can grow, but they certainly create a wealth of types whom we can love or despise—fathers and children, sons and lovers, matchmakers, shopworkers, and ladies of leisure. And, in another way, the very form in which these letters are arranged, by social situation and relationship,

---

5. New York, Saperstein and Katzenelenbogen, 1892.

and their function as models of how to write one's own hesitant letters to a spouse or an employer clearly would have had an effect on one's perception of oneself and of one's circumstances. The effect would have been to lend these letters a post facto authenticity all their own.

Beyond a sense of authenticity is the dramatic quality that *Blaustein's Brivenshteler* creates by its recurrent cycles of letter-and-reply, sometimes amounting to vignettes with their own suspense and dénouement and their own development of character and style.

But not a hint of this is in the preface. The anonymous author deplores existing *Brivenshtelers* for their "lack of taste," for using "expressions that are not for young children . . . ," for emptiness, or for "exhuberant turns of phrase and flowery flights of fancy like the third plague in Egypt" (in simple words, "crawling with them"). Considered altogether, they aren't "practical or useful."

HISTORY OF *BLAUSTEIN'S BRIVENSHTELER*

Blaustein's Brivenshteler was published in Warsaw by Aaron Tseylengold. To judge by the dates chosen for the letters it contains—Warsaw, 5 November 1903; Minsk, 8 November 1903; and so on—it apparently appeared in 1903 or 1904, as is supported by the poignant references in letter 54 to the Kishinev pogroms of April 1903. The title page describes it as [my translation] a "Yiddish teacher, printed and handwritten letters, various useful skills, calculation, etiquette and deportment, important and necessary for any class for learning to write pure Yiddish [*reyn zhargon*], to read and reckon. In four parts, composed from new sources and edited by author H.Sh.N." The letters make up the second part, amounting to two-thirds of the whole book. They are reproduced here in their entirety, with the exception of a handful of dull commercial letters.[6]

The whole work then seems to have promptly migrated to America. A version in an elegant Yiddish font, but with thirty-two letters removed for no obvious reason (and with a curious change of "America" to "Africa" in letters 17 and 18), was published in 1905 by the Hebrew Publishing Company of New York; the dates and places of the letters were similarly omitted. Subsequently, the book was reproduced in its original form under the title *Steinberg's Brivenshteler* (presumably taken from the name of the imaginary author of the first letter) by the Star Publishing Company of New York, and then was once again acquired by the Hebrew Publishing Company, who continued to print it until recent years.[7]

---

6. The absence of the date and place in letters 64–82 is because these letters have been torn out of the copy of the Warsaw edition in my possession. The American reprint omits date and place.

7. I am grateful to Professor Joseph Bar-El and to Ms. Dina Abramowicz of YIVO for making available to me the Warsaw and the Star Publishing Company versions, respectively.

THE *BRIVENSHTELER* AND THE GENRE(S) OF THE LETTER MANUAL

In its long history, the European letter-writing manual has served a variety of goals, broadly evolving[8] as follows:

- "Formulary": a book of rules for administrative and scholarly correspondence in Latin
- "Academy": model letters and rules, expanded to include lovers' letters
- "Secretary": moralizing letters telling stories to instruct merchants and the middle classes
- "Textbook": moralizing stories, sometimes threaded into full-scale novels, for the nineteenth-century school

Blaustein's Brivenshteler clearly has some of the features of a "Secretary": It is short on rules and consists mostly of letters that tell tales, speaking to the concerns of the adult reader and, in its final section, to those of young people.

However, while the tone is in certain parts moralizing, more often than not the letters simply have a "human interest" effect—informative or dramatic. What precisely was the author trying to achieve with this little book that claimed to offer impoverished Jewish migrants "practical and useful" models for writing letters in "pure Yiddish" (when most Jews would have denied such a thing

---

8. Jean Robertson, *The Art of Letter Writing* (London: Hodder & Stoughton, 1943).

existed)? And why, one finds oneself asking, has a Yiddish letter-writing manual come to be so full of human interest?

Here, the studies by Thomas Beebee on the development of stories-by-letter, epistolary fiction, are particularly instructive.[9] Beebee argues that the "necessary basis" of all letter-writing manuals in recent centuries has been the narrative. At one end of the spectrum, this may just be a matter of "short flights of fiction"; at the other, it may swell into a "master narrative," as happened for the first time with Samuel Richardson's epistolary novel *Pamela*, which arose from the 138th and 139th letters of his letter-writing manual ("A father to a daughter in service on hearing her Master's attempting her Virtue" and "the Daughter's answer"). The raison d'être of this storyline, in the case of letter manuals, is most likely that they have commonly sought to educate, in the broader sense, "that the letters may serve for rules to THINK and ACT by, as well as FORMS to WRITE after" (Richardson). After all, business letters aside, writing a letter primarily served to project the relationship of the correspondents to one another and to society, seeking to reinforce or reform—"social positioning," in Beebee's words, outweighing "rhetorical positioning." And there was nothing quite so potent an educator as a moral tale. A further function

---

9. See, in particular, Thomas Beebee, *The Ideology of Genre* (Philadelphia: Penn State University Press, 1994) and *The Genealogy of Epistolary Fiction* (Philadelphia: Penn State University Press, in press).

of the storyline is to create a sheer sense of structure and regularity.

The moral tale may, of course, be impersonal—an allegory, for example, or a common topos like "The Repentant Son." But from the mid-eighteenth century onward, the individual comes to the fore, and in the letter manual as well. Time and place, too, will be individualized. The outcome may be a virtual documentary, with the letters creating a form of "authentic" discourse. And nineteenth-century French school letter manuals actually sought to promote spontaneity, in the tradition of Mme. de Sévigné's view that written style should echo natural speech. From this, it is a short leap to an epistolary novel shorn of didactic intent or authorial presence, a thoroughly documentary novel, such as Amos Oz's *Black Box*.[10]

Besides or instead of an ethical message, the letter manual might have a political message. As Janet Gurkin Altman has noted,[11] it "projected a code of representation" and "a political unconscious" in an age that lacked other mass media. While the surface structure of the manual might be a social one, with divisions according to kinship, age, occupation, or other social standing, the deep message might be a quite different, political one—for example, the power of wealth or patronage.

All these forces may well be pulling together at

---

10. Amos Oz, *Black Box* (London: Chatto & Windus, 1988).

11. Janet Gurkin Altman, "Political Ideology in the Letter Manual," *Studies in Eighteenth Century Culture* 18 (1989), pp. 105–122.

Introduction

any one time, to create a permanent, but not unwanted, conflict between *ars*, the technical functions of the manual, and the creative functions.

Beyond Beebee's theory of the letter manual, one has to consider the fictive potential of the very act of writing a letter. Claudio Guillen has recently suggested that the letter should be viewed as "moving along a continuum that may reach or shift or combine three main levels or categories of achievement: literacy, literariness, and poeticity." And he goes on: "There is hardly an act in our daily experience . . . as likely as the writing of a letter to propel us towards inventiveness and the interpretation and transformation of fact."[12]

All this casts a very different light on our own *Brivenshteler*. In venturing into the realm of moral and ethical education and "human interest" narrative, *Blaustein's Brivenshteler* may be seen not as a peculiar "blip" but as part of a European tradition—even as an organic outcome of the genre of letter-writing manuals *per se*. It is also significant that the title page and preface of the Warsaw edition, in which the author or publisher tries so hard to sell the book, makes no mention whatsoever of its moral, literary, or documentary qualities.[13] He surely cannot be taking them for granted.

---

12. Claudio Guillen, "On the Edge of Literariness: The Writing of Letters," *Comparative Literature Studies* 31 (1994), pp. 1–24.

13. Similarly, the title page of the 1905 New York edition simply states (my translation): "Letter writing manual with handwriting script. Comprises various short letters for children, various letters for family and friendship, love letters,

Might they instead be the author's own indulgence, which neither he nor his publishers felt should publicly be acknowledged—in short, a kind of conspiracy with the readership? If the kind of fiction in our *Brivenshteler* was felt to need masking as educational matter, it appears that it was intended not only for women (they had no compunction about reading Yiddish fiction openly) but also for a large segment of the Jewish male population: the partially schooled,[14] who could not write Yiddish without recourse to a manual, but who would have felt it frivolous and even a touch illicit to read patent fiction. We say "frivolous" rather than "immoral," for this manual, containing children's letters, would obviously have been read by children. The reading of any but the most moralizing fiction was widely felt to be *bitel zman*, "time wasting," an offense against the Jewish male's traditional duty

---

and business letters. Also rules for reading, and necessary Hebrew words and abbreviations used in written Yiddish."

14. See Shaul Stampfer, "Literacy among Eastern European Jewry in the Modern Period: Context, Background, and Implications," in *Transition and Change in Modern Jewish History: Essays Presented in Honor of Shmuel Ettinger*, Shmuel Almog et al., eds. (Jerusalem: Historical Society of Israel, 1987), pp. 459-483, who underlines the differences between reading and writing literacy and observes that the *heder* did not generally teach writing skills, and many Jews were doing manual work that did not require an ability to write. Indeed, a 1901 survey of Minsk Jews revealed that one-third of younger women and one-quarter of younger men could not even read their language. A set of surveys of Jewish arrivals in the United States done in 1913 showed that between 15 percent and 40 percent of women could not read Yiddish.

to devote his spare time to the study of Torah. To read it in Yiddish was a double embarrassment, as formal Yiddish had hitherto generally been regarded as a women's language—men ought to be reading Hebrew, at least according to the popular stereotype. The ethnographers Zborowski and Herzog have portrayed the scene as the book peddler came into town:[15]

> "The girls come running, shoving and crowding to get first chance as he cries: 'Books for women and sacred books for men.' The 'books' are in Yiddish and the 'sacred books' in Hebrew."

But the book peddler's cry evokes the stereotype, while for the reality[16] the ethnographers refer one to the epitaph on the grave of Sholem Aleichem:

> "Here lies a Jew, a simple one,
> He wrote in Yiddish for women
> And for the *prosteh* [simple] folk he was
> A humorist, a writer."

---

15. Zborowski and Herzog, op. cit., pp. 126-127. For a radical perspective on the stereotyping of Yiddish, and of *shtetl* life in general, as "feminine" and "feeble," see Christopher Hutton, "Freud and the Family Drama of Yiddish," in *Studies in Yiddish Linguistics*, Paul Wexler, ed. (Tübingen: Max Niemeyer Verlag, 1990), pp. 9-22.

16. For some indication of how much Yiddish was in fact used as a serious written medium for propagating the message of early Hasidism, see Naftali Loewenthal, "Hebrew and the *Habad* Communication Ethos," in *Hebrew in Ashkenaz: A Language in Exile*, Lewis Glinert, ed. (New York: Oxford University Press, 1993), pp. 167-193, especially pp. 167-168.

Equally striking, many of the events portrayed in this letter manual are bound up with the mass Jewish migrations across the Pale of Settlement or across the seas. "Why have I not heard from you in so long?" or "Come to us and live a better life" are recurrent themes. Life itself seems to hang from letters, from people's willingness to write them and their sheer ability to do this. Was there ever another letter manual, one wonders, in which this was so acutely true? And this, too, is sublimated within the bland form of a manual.

The following sections broadly illustrate the major themes and functions of the letters in our *Brivenshteler*.

Structure

The letters are arranged in eleven sets, reflecting their functions and the social relationships involved. One-third are (adult) family letters; another third are letters for courtship, fiancés, and spouses; and the remainder are mostly for friends and children. Very few letters are classed by function alone: a handful for matchmaking, invitation, and congratulation—and one solitary letter of condolence (only introduced in the 1905 edition). There are also ten business letters, which we have omitted.

If the number of "function" letters is strikingly small, the explanation may lie in the remarkable fact that nearly all the letters are actually in pairs: Approach + Response (e.g., Father to Son and Reply, Shimon to Naomi and Naomi to Shimon).

This repartee is clearly designed to create the narrative or dramatic character that appears to be the manual's raison d'être, and invitations, condolences, business letters, and the like would not contribute to this goal.

The Narrative Within

The hidden author(s) did not stop at a simple "two-move" repartee. Six exchanges involve three or four letters (e.g., Rosa and Isaac, letters 62–64; Pinchas and Perl, letters 65–67), while the exchange between the brothers Solomon and Wolf, letters 17–22, and Anna and Phillip's courtship, letters 37–42, are six-letter "rallies."

This creates some full-blown vignettes and short stories. Thus, the six-letter interchange between the upbeat Solomon in the United States and his distressed brother Wolf in the Old Country paints a conflict and a quandary that faced so many Jews in 1903: whether to leave and arrive practically penniless on foreign shores? Or to stay on and hope for better times that might well never come? The final letter in the series leaves us in suspense: Will Wolf take the plunge?

The exchange in letters 29–32 between Rosa in Libava (Latvia) and her sister Lina in Yekaterinoslav portrays the latter as a place where "from morning to night people wear themselves out earning their crust of bread." It ends with Lina plucking up the courage to migrate to Latvia and strike a blow for womanly enterprise by opening a workshop in her sister's town.

The depiction of the courtship between Anna and Phillip, in letters 37-42, struggles with Anna's dilemma of whether and how to broach her parents. The climax comes when Phillip presents two alternatives: asking her parents himself or going through a matchmaker. The final letter brings quite an unexpected and dramatically elegant dénouement: her mother discovers the correspondence, but inadvertently rather than by prying. Yet, far from causing their downfall, it leads to their parents' approval, since they know Phillip's family anyway.

The overall impression is that if the author(s) had taken the step of intertwining the various actions, one would have had the rudiments of a Yiddish novel.

The Ethos of the Book

The ethos of Jewish life in a rapidly changing Eastern Europe—its tone and quality of life, its moral and aesthetic style—comes across powerfully in our *Brivenshteler*. Almost every letter has been invested with a real-life situation or attitude or value. The author's values are sometimes evident in the names he gives the correspondents, but—remarkably, perhaps, for lowbrow literature of this type—the combined effect of the exchanges is not a strong moralizing tone but more frequently a balance between the various moral and pragmatic choices. Conflict abounds. A generation was deserting not only its traditional lifestyle and values but also its traditional lands;[17] several of the letters are set in America or England.

The perceptions of a single author cannot, of course, be said to represent the mores of a generation or even a generation's stereotypes of itself; but there is no denying the effect that *Brivenshtelers* had on the untutored masses, who were helped in crystallizing their own thoughts.

Boy finds girl in a bewildering variety of ways.[18] Letters 87-90 show the traditional system operating—*shadchen* ("matchmaker") and parents initiate proceedings, and the children follow up. In letter 87 a wealthy father asks a *shadchen* to find a match for his daughter; the *shadchen* eagerly responds. In letter 89 it is the *shadchen* who approachs the father of the girl, and the father responds. (Both exchanges are revealing as to the relative weight of looks, money, character, and family in the equation, as well as to the stereotytpe of the *shadchen*.) However, letters 91 and 92 show the system beginning to come apart—not in some industrial new world like Lodz or Warsaw but in the backwaters of Grodno and Bialistok. The *shadchen* is still

---

17. Compare, for example, Lucy S. Davidowicz, ed. *The Golden Tradition: Jewish Life and Thought in Eastern Europe* (New York: Holt, Rinehart and Winston, 1967) and Irving Howe, *World of Our Fathers* (New York: Simon and Schuster, 1976).

18. A perceptive discussion of the ethos behind these particular letters, and the only analysis known to me of Yiddish *Brivenshteler* material, is Nathan Hurvitz, "Courtship and Arranged Marriages Among Eastern European Jews Prior to World War I as Depicted in a *Briefenshteller*," *Journal of Marriage and the Family* 37 (1975), pp. 422-430.

there, but now it is the young suitor who approaches him, with protestations of love, and asks him to bring both sets of parents into the arrangement—a very different brand of "arranged marriage"! The *shadchen* is quite happy to abet this change. There is nothing of Romeo and Juliet in this exchange. The young couple have been able to meet and fall in love (certainly not an unusual thing in traditional life), and they sound sanguine about their prospects.

The traditional system has retreated still further in letters 37-42. Here, there is no *shadchen* whatsoever. At issue is whether or not to consult one's parents at all concerning marriage. Again, this is not New York or Warsaw but Grodno and Bialistok. Phillip and Anna are two young people whose very names breathe modernity. They have clearly had opportunities to get to know one another socially without their parents' involvement, conceivably at work or at a club. Phillip's debonair opening gambit sounds as if it could have come from any drawing room in Berlin or Boston. But Anna replies: "In my case, it happens that parents deserve not to be dispensed with for such a step as this." And he concurs, but still says, "I do not have patience enough to await their happy acquiescence." She protests, yet says, "I am just not so brazen as to suggest such a thing to my good parents—this is too difficult an undertaking for a woman. Advise me how it should happen." By her own actions she has rebelled against arranged marriage, but she cannot face the outcome of her actions. He then offers her a choice of plans: that he ask her parents himself, or they revert to the old ways of asking a *shadchen*. The crisis is resolved when her parents learn of the liaison and affirm that they know and approve of Phillip's family. The narrative thus offers an elegant way—fortuitous, admittedly—of compromising between Anna's instincts for arranged marriage and Phillip's initial desire for independent choice. Observe that the net effect of these letters is not a strong moral adjudication but an implicit endorsement of a new middle way. The young couple's own choice of partner is vindicated by their parents' acquaintance with the other family; the couple's reservations about going behind their parents' back are rewarded; and, in not condemning the secrecy of the liaison but approving the outcome, the parents seem implicitly to approve the new role of the family as giving final endorsement on the basis of a thorough acquaintance.

Parents and family acquaintance are altogether out of the picture in letters 50 and 51, set in Latvia, away from the traditional heartland. Sonia has been betrayed by her "depraved" fiancé after three years of "passionate love." Her friend Fanye claims "we warned you," but this was not sufficient. Whether the old system would have protected her better is not an issue in this exchange—the implication is "Girls beware!"

And from Latvia to America, in letter 73, an instant marriage for Tanya—no three years of passionate love: "We met one another at a wedding, he liked me and—like an American, without any rigmarole—he asked for my hand and that was that." In the exchange that ensues with her friend Clara, America gets full marks. There is no hint of wariness or problems like those in letters 50 and

51, unless there is faint implied criticism in the words "My fiancé is handsome, wealthy, and kind. Here one does not go by education—one has to be a *mentsh*, capable in business and in running a household, and he is absolutely all of that."

Other aspects of traditional *Yiddishkeit* ("Jewishness") are also changing. The letters depict old-style Jewish education in the throes of a revolution that was liable to destroy it. Perl Gilbo writes in letter 66 of the old-style and the new-style *melamed* ("tutor"). To her, as to her husband, the old *melamed* in the Old Country "might just as well be dumb," as long as he had long *peyes* (sidelocks) and knew a bit . . . But a new breed of *melamed* was arising. In place of *peyes* he might just as easily be dressed modern, dandy even, as long as he knew Russian and Hebrew, to satisfy the demands of both the Russian authorities (determined to "assimilate" the Jew) and the new, acculturating Jewish masses, for whom Jewish education was rapidly becoming—as it has long been in the West—a matter of Hebrew texts rather than Torah lifestyle. "I must tell you," Perl writes to her reluctant husband, "that the name *melamed* no longer has a stigma attached to it. . . . But it has already become the fashion today that you should not call yourself *melamed* but *lerer*, call yourself whatever suits you, just earn some money." Should one cheer or weep?

But there is a further ambivalent twist in this bitter vignette. Pinchas takes the job, but far from it being a pushover, he has to admit: "I guess I will never figure out how human health can cope with teaching twenty to thirty children like the *melameds* do." This, of course, does not mean that the work holds any dignity for him, the kind of dignity that comes from hoeing a field or oiling an engine. His final dig at the profession has probably never been surpassed: "Write and tell me if they accept a *melamed*'s money, too."

Remarkably, there is hardly a hint of secularism in the letters. Questioning of ritual observance or religious belief is absent, despite the acute practical dilemmas that such matters as Sabbath observance or *kashrut* posed for so many Jews. Very possibly, our *Brivenshteler* is evidence that a broad section of Jewry-on-the-move no longer considered these to be concerns of high profile.

It is, however, instructive that traditional Jewish sentiments are often lacking. Thus the author of the letter of condolence, number 102, while hoping that God will support the bereaved, disregards the tradition of the *hesped* ("eulogy") and says almost nothing in praise of the deceased; nor are the traditional Hebrew words of comfort (*Hamokem yenachem oyscho . . .*) mentioned or even alluded to. There is, however, a biblical quotation, which smacks more of the *Haskalah* than of the *shtetl*: *Imcho onoychi betsoro* ("I am with you in your grief.")

One Jewish tradition is conspicuous by its absence: On the occasion of an engagement or wedding, instead of being wished the time-hallowed blessings of establishing a solid home and having children who will perform *mitzves* ("precepts") and grow up to stand under the *chupe* ("wedding canopy"), et cetera, it is remarkable how often the young couple are wished "everything you wish yourselves" (e.g., letters 34 and 101). There is something rather detached and modern about this all-purpose, "modular" greeting.

Another prominent moral issue of the times is wealth and ostentation. There is conflict in the homes of the nouveau-riche. Rosa enjoys consorting with "respectable" (as she calls them) high-spending ladies whose greatest pleasure is to say they have bankrupted their husbands, but her husband writes to her irately in letter 63: "We are no millionaires, no empty aristocrats who buy their aristocracy from high designers and in the off-the-peg stores. We are ordinary people; I do not 'wish' to go bust, nor will I with God's help."

It is also at the spas that Jewish women are subject to the exotic lures of the Gentile male. Lisa Kalmensohn, in letter 72, is intent on making this very evident when she writes to her husband about her aversion to coming home at all. "I have had very nice company here, particularly a neighbor of mine, a nice young German, never in my life have I met such a person. He left today already." But our potential Jewish Madame Bovary ends on the same note as all the other Esthers and Perels: "Send me as much money as you can."

Letter 70, an emotional letter from a friend recalling old days, describes an era when borrowing from friends was more normal than borrowing from a bank or maybe even from the community.

In general, these letters are a window on the nature of personal interactions and relationships. Letter 64 illustrates sentiments of simple devotion between friends: "For me it is a festival when I receive a letter from you, and when I write you a letter, too." Sentiments are often melodramatic by today's Western standards. People are not loath to squeeze the last ounce of advantage out of relationships, be they of blood or of water. Thus, a friend's invitation to a wedding (letter 97) begins: "A time has come when you can show me how far your friendship with me extends, and how well you remember me—my elder son will be getting married, please God, in ten days (may it turn out well). . . ." There is here a hint of the compelling ties of obligation so prevalent in pre-modern societies and still observed in Asian immigrant communities in the United States and Britain.[19]

The Economic and Political Situation

The bulk of the letters are set in Eastern Europe, most of them in the traditional Jewish heartland but a fair number in the expanding Jewish areas of Latvia. A few are written from the United States (there is mention of Chicago, New York, and Boston) and even from England and South Africa. Not surprisingly for these times of migration, the letters have much to say about economic and political circumstances and about perceptions and stereotypes.

Letter 21, for example, brings home the economic quandary faced by so many Eastern European Jews longing to escape: ". . . but such a trip takes money; and the only money I can make is

---

19. See, for example, Alison Shaw, *A Pakistani Community in Britain* (Oxford: Blackwell, 1988).

from my house, if I were to sell it, but there are no dealers now, no one wants to put money into a house. Everyone would rather be a rich tenant than a poor homeowner. So, what can one do?"

Relief was sometimes gained by internal migration. Letter 86 actually describes the way in which a *shtetl* formed: "I have left Lyutsin for Korsovka, to date a village where Jews were not allowed to live, meaning to settle. But it has now turned into a small township, and our fellow Jews have moved in from many cities, where they live, poor wretches, packed together like herrings in a barrel."

Letter 65 describes "the worst of all possible things" economically: "becoming a *melamed* (a 'tutor')". Pinchas is faced with tutoring three children in a village in exchange for bed, board, and twenty rubles per month, a paltry wage and a shameful job.

Letter 54 refers directly to the pogroms of Kishinev of 1903, but through a mother's anguish at visiting the grave of her murdered son three months after the events. Her husband's letter reacts in a remarkable way. Without so much as a mention of their son's death or their anguish, he describes the way in which he is earning a living and the technicalities by which he will be sending money, and then he implores his wife to use the ticket he is sending her to join him in an America in which "a Jew can also live," where "everyone is safe, everyone is equal." Although we know what a frightening impact the pogroms had upon Jews around the world, we sense here an exhilaration that America was, as letter 21 puts it, "the latter-day Land of Israel, a place where you can earn money by your efforts, where work is rewarded, and where every human being can engage in whatever he wishes and wherever he so wishes"—an unwitting (or witting?) echo of the Puritan conception of the New America. Let us quote again from letter 73 on the business and domestic ethos of the United States as opposed to Europe: "Here one does not go by education—one has to be a *mentsh*, capable in business and in running a household. . . ."

The British and their dominions come off with mixed marks in letter 77 from South Africa: "You must already have assumed that I have become a perfect Englishman and have no shame about lying . . ."

Sometimes we find a dogged determination to be satisfied with the *shtetl*. In letter 80: "It usually comes nowhere near the living you make in New York, but we countryfolk are satisfied with what we have." But sometimes there is a weariness and a wish to quit: (letter 78) "I toil like a mule and I get what Pharaoh got . . . Just you make yourself a living there and we will correspond, maybe I will also go to Africa." Letter 19 states: "things are indeed dire—we cannot even derive much joy from the children, although they are bright. Forgive me, my dear brother, for singing such a lonesome song—'You sing the song of the wagon you're on . . .'" And letter 19, by a Jew in the Old Country to a brother in the New: "I have at last received a letter from you, and, thank God, a very happy one. I must tell you quite frankly, brother, that I cannot write such good things about myself. But I do not want you to think I am an exception! I think that here in our part of the world, there is not a Jew who makes a decent living. We all live off air. . . ."

The reactions and self-perceptions of the Jews who made it to the New World are by no means simple. Take letter 81: "You write that your life in the country does not come up to my life in New York. There is nothing one has less need of than to live in a great city. You do not live like you would want, everything seems to have been made by machine, even running a household. . . . No, my dear friend, there is nothing to be envious of."

There is an expectation that Jews in America might forget about the life they had left, in letter 20: "It surprises you that in the course of eighteen years I have not forgotten about Jewish life or about your sweat and toil; some surprise!"

THE TONE OF THE BOOK

While our *Brivenshteler* tends to steer a neutral course amid the lifestyles and values it depicts, there are elements of satire or just plain humor.

Certain names signed to the letters are in this category—sometimes they are merely cute and sometimes mordant, while often quite imaginative. There is Helena Glueckswuensch ("good luck wish"), Anna Scheinfinkel ("spark of beauty"), Ber Lieberman ("dear man"), Zalman Neuhaus ("new home"—on an invitation to a circumcision), Isaac Eisenstein ("man of iron"—with a letter of condolence), Leon Gampyofitz (based on *ma yofis zingen*, "to suck up," the name of a scoundrel described by his ex-fiancée as "depraved" and "base"), and Rosa Shochadkewitz (*shochad* means "bribery"—

from her seashore hotel she sends her husband a peremptory demand for sending money and lots of it).

Letter 81 gives us a Sholem Aleychem-type of logical rigmarole: "My daughter, who is getting married, says that she deserves a thank-you. If she had not wanted her future husband, she would not be a bride-to-be, and if she were not a bride-to-be, I would not have invited you to a wedding and would perhaps not yet have made up my mind to write to you."

Occasionally, it is a comical type of person that is being mocked. There is the matchmaker, of course. And letter 62 depicts the wife who wants her husband to send her just a few eentsy-weentsy little things that she's forgotten to take on vacation with her: "I am short of three items and then I will have everything—four nice, good dresses, a rain coat, a few bathing costumes, an iron, a white silk parasol, and the like. You understand, of course, that I need money besides, as everything here is costly, only money is cheap. . . ." And the delicious irony in her concluding thought: "I am sure you will only be able to come out here in a few weeks, so dispatch me money for everything as soon as you possibly can."

WHAT KIND OF YIDDISH IS THIS?

To many of those who have campaigned for "pure Yiddish," the language of the letters in our *Brivenshteler* is liable to raise some hackles. In their spelling, vocabulary, and style, they have many of the typical features of turn-of-the-century "germanization."

The penetration of a wave of modern standard Germanisms (*daytshmerish*) into Yiddish at the time of the mass migrations was, and still is, the subject of intense controversy. The American Yiddish author Leon Kobrin[20] has recalled how "pseudo-germanized Yiddish was then a sign of refined taste, of a cultured taste, so to speak. One needs only to remind oneself of the language of the old-time Yiddish letters that Jewish boys and girls— and ordinary Jewish women of a certain type— used to write when they wanted to demonstrate their 'modernity' and education." Irving Howe, describing the first generation of Eastern European migrants, writes "The writers had barely any tradition by which to temper their work; the very language they used was unsettled, a Yiddish coarsened with Germanisms and syntactically insecure . . ."[21] But this was not merely the expression of an immature pen. A large segment of the American and Eastern European Jewish press favored this "pseudo-germanized" Yiddish; so, too, did the Yiddish theater of the day, in part to paper over the differences between the various Yiddish dialects. Meanwhile, more serious authors sought instead to echo the "simple language that one's mother spoke," to use Alexander Harkavy's expression. And this "simple language" was set up as a model

---

20. Leon Kobrin, "From '*Daytchmerish*' to Yiddish in America," originally published in 1944 and in an English version in *Yiddish* 2 (1976), pp. 39–48.

21. Op. cit., p. 418.

for "pure Yiddish," a seeming contradiction in terms and an open challenge to the many Jews brought up to look down on Yiddish as mere *Zhargon*. Of course, as sociologists of language have noted,[22] the gap is wide between what people say about their language and what they actually do. And in the hands of serious authors or even journalists, the "simple language that one's mother spoke" was, of course, elaborate and complicated; but at the root of the quest for "pure Yiddish" was a desire to distance oneself in certain select ways from what were perceived as the worst modern Germanisms. This was a quest for a distinct linguistic identity, expressed not only in vocabulary and style but also in pronunciation and spelling.

In some circles, this quest for distinct identity led to the creation of a standard that has had far-reaching influence in the promotion of Yiddish. First, in the 1930s, mounting concern arose in Eastern Europe that a modern language without a uniform literary standard is bound to suffer grievously in competition with the standardized languages of the Gentiles. Then, following World War II, philologists of the YIVO Institute for Jewish Research in New York dedicated to the rescue of Yiddish proceeded to enshrine particular norms of pronunciation, grammar, vocabulary, and orthography in such works as Uriel Weinreich's *College Yiddish* and *Modern English–Yiddish Yiddish–English Dictionary*. All manner of words that might

---

22. See, for example, Joshua A. Fishman, *Language and Nationalism* (Rowley, Mass.: Newbury House, 1972).

have been regarded as Yiddish by many Yiddish speakers, such as *yetst* or *boychik*, were delegitimized as Germanisms or Anglicisms.

But this is just one point of view. Viewed from a broader perspective, a century later, when Yiddish is no longer the language in which most Jews can write a sentence—let alone a whole message—these letters have a linguistic charm all their own. They are a tangible testimony of how the Jewish masses expressed themselves when they sat down to write a letter, the "old-time Yiddish letters that Jewish boys and girls—and ordinary Jewish women of a certain type—used to write when they wanted to demonstrate their 'modernity' and education," as Kobrin put it. They are, of course, concoctions, not authentic acts of communication. But they served as a model of Yiddish writing for the masses; and for a public that was not generally schooled in writing Yiddish, they no doubt had a profound effect. Well might the guardians of Yiddish have lyricized about how the common folk talked their *Mame Loshn*, but when common folk *wrote* to their uncles or fiancés or even to their spouses, they would naturally aspire to a more fussy, not to say pompous, form of Yiddish. This was, after all, in an age when formal written communication throughout Europe was far removed from casual oral communication, and, indeed, oral vernaculars were widely considered contemptible.[23] In fact, until the mid-nineteenth century,

---

23. On the role of written language in Europe, see Walter J. Ong, *Orality and Literacy: The Technologizing of the Word* (London and New York: Methuen, 1985).

Jewish men had been accustomed to use another language entirely for formal writing—Hebrew.[24]

A further linguistic attraction of such letter-writing manuals is that they were also a form of popular literature, a series of narratives in their own right; as such, they again command the interest that is due nowadays to popular literature of all types. In much the same way, we may find the style of English used in 1905 in the magazines and potboilers stashed away in our grandparents' attics to be odd, clumsy, common perhaps—but it speaks to us.

And even when viewed from the narrower perspective of "pure Yiddish" and "correct models," the Yiddish of these letters should not be dismissed out-of-hand for its Germanisms. As Dovid Katz has recently argued,[25] which modern Germanisms are deemed part of Yiddish and which are excluded is ultimately bound to be a matter of vox populi, and not a matter of logic or of academic or literary preference. Clearly, even Yiddish purists

---

24. The symbiosis between "low-function" Yiddish and "high-function" Hebrew, known as "diglossia," has been portrayed by Joshua Fishman, *Yiddish: Turning to Life* (Amsterdam: John Benjamins, 1991) and Israel Bartal, "From Traditional Bilingualism to National Monolingualism," in *Hebrew in Ashkenaz: A Language in Exile*, Lewis Glinert, ed. (New York: Oxford University Press, 1993), pp. 141–150.

25. Dovid Katz, *Tikney Takones* (Amended Amendments: Issues in Yiddish Stylistics) (Oxforder Yiddish Press, Oxford, 1993), especially pp. 166–185. On nineteenth-century Yiddish written style in general, see Dovid Roskies, "*Yidishe shraybshprakhn in nayntsentn yorhundert*," *Yidishe Shprakh* 33 (1974), pp 1–11.

have never had problems with words like *kultur* or *frage* or with other modern Germanisms *per se*. Indeed, a westernized vocabulary has always been happily accepted as part and parcel of the westernization of the old Jewish lifestyle. And if one looks beyond the purists to the Yiddish that the best authors or the average Jew employed, one finds many other Germanisms happily absorbed, for no compelling reason, into the body of Yiddish. Among words that Weinreich's *Dictionary* labels as "of doubtful admissibility in the standard language" are *eynike*, "a few"; *oyser*, "besides"; *onshtendik*, "respectable"; *antdeken*, "discover"; *art*, "type"; and *beishpil*, "example"—all regarded by Dovid Katz as "good Yiddish words,"[26] and all regularly used in our *Brivenshteler*.

However, it would be doing scant justice to this letter-writing manual to cast it, as such manuals are wont to be cast, as a thoughtless collection of faked letters penned by anonymous hacks. Our *Brivenshteler* is, in fact, a sensitive reflector of the sociolinguistic life of a language. Whoever composed these letters was able to convey a wealth of places, lifestyles, outlooks, and relationships, and his own attitude to them—and to convey them by the subtlest of lexical or grammatical means—at a time when Jewish life was in social turmoil.

Let us take just a few examples. Courland, today part of the Baltic republic of Latvia, had a distinctively Germanic ethos and culture, and Courland Jews were well-known for their *Haskalah* leanings

---

26. Katz, ibid., p. 188.

Introduction

and the germanized Yiddish that they spoke. Letter 24, purportedly from Courland, is duly infused with germanized grammar.

The highly germanized *und* for *un* in letter 35 betrays Max, the future brother-in-law, as a social climber. The form in which Anna Scheinfinkel signs off in the correspondence (letters 38, 40, and 42) that leads to her engagement—first, with the authentic Yiddish *eier Ana*, but then with the germanized feminine inflection *eiere Ana*—seems even grammatically to echo and betoken the "liberation" of a young couple set on acculturating to European society, still concerned enough to ask their parents' consent and even, if necessary, to use the traditional matchmaker to engineer this final act of consent, but keenly aware that their fate is "in their own hands." In this same letter, the shift from the conjunction *az* to the more germanized *dos* when Anna reaches the climax of her account, her consultation with her parents, appears to reflect a heightened sense of formality, or even cultural accommodation, at that point.

However, to view germanization without reference to the concomitant trend to de-hebraization is to misread the sociolinguistic dynamics of the situation. Time and time again in these letters, we find that it is the traditional Hebraic components of Yiddish[27] that are being usurped by modern Germanisms—and although many Hebraisms were

---

27. On the origin and character of Hebrew in Yiddish, see, for example, Dovid Katz, "Hebrew, Aramaic, and the Rise of Yiddish," in *Readings in the Sociology of Jewish Languages*, Joshua A. Fishman, ed. (Leiden: E.J. Brill, 1985), pp. 85–103.

associated with displays of religious scholarship and were not missed by large sections of society,[28] many others were part of the folk culture that created a sense of Jewish identity and solidarity. Thus, the usage of *broytigam* and *broyte* in letters 34–36, in place of *chosen* and *kale*—and at that very time vying to usurp the latter—is a mirror of changes in the acculturation of Eastern European Jews. Similarly, letter 74 from a girl in Europe to a girlfriend getting married in modern style in the United States asks when the *hochtseit*, rather than the *chasene*, will be. The word *chasene* is nevertheless used by her American friend, talking about someone *else's* wedding, where she first met her husband-to-be. A mere chance, or a subtle sociolinguistic feature, betokening a desire to "accommodate" culturally? Notice, too, that she begins her letter with an out-and-out Germanism marked by a German verbal suffix, *-e: ich gratulire dir*. In letter 40 we see *englen, rat* being suggested in place of *maluchim, eytse*—and, in the case of "angels," with thoroughly Gentile ideas in mind: the two angels are "Hope" and "Future," the one perhaps traditional and classical but the other unmistakably modern. In letter 33 we see *farlobung* being recommended in place of *tnoim*. Letter 70, written from a spa, talks of the high society doctors there as *ertste* (German: *Ärzte*), rather than the standard

---

28. Thus, Howe (op. cit., p. 430) describes the modernist group of poets, the *Yunge*, who "were also chary in using hebraisms, because they knew that for a Yiddish writer to employ a biblical phrase or rabbinical reference can often be a lazy substitute for discovering his own image."

Hebraic-Yiddish *doktoyrim*. In letter 72 Lisa Kalmensohn, describing the society at the spa that she is so reluctant to leave, talks about her handsome young German neighbor not as her *shochen* but as her *nachbar*.

Letter 53, the letter from Russia by a wife to a husband, has an Old Country ring about it, with its many Hebraisms—*meshiech, bekoved, tsore, mishpet, cheyn gefinen, im yirtse Hashem*—despite the imaginary writer's clear attempt to dissociate herself from *di frume*, "the religious people." Here, too, we see a modernism, *shef*, being recommended for *balebos fun gesheft*. Contrast the exchange between the two brothers Wolf (in Europe) and Solomon (in the United States) in letters 19 and 20: the word *nigen* (*ich zing mit azoy an umediken nigen*) with the word *lid* (*dein umedike lid*).

Other Hebraisms avoided are *mishpoche* (instead, *familye*), *mazel*, and *mazeldik* (instead, *glik* and *gliklech*).

Further indication that Hebraisms and Judaic turns of phrase had a folksy ring about them comes from the way that they tend to go hand-in-hand with a more graphic, racy vocabulary—for example, a word like *ployderzak*, "windbag," in letter 96. Alluding to the *nusech* (the "wording," a Hebraism) of the letter of reference he sent concerning a possible marriage, he says [I have underlined the Hebraisms or religious phrases]: *Ich farshtey az dos hot forgeleygt a <u>sochrisher</u> mentsh, nit a ployderzak a shadchen. Gib Got dos zol mit <u>mazel</u> oysgefirt vern, in <u>a gute sho</u>.* ("I understand that it has been proposed by someone businesslike, not a windbag of a matchmaker. Please God, it may be brought to completion under a lucky star.")

Sometimes, the letters of East European origin explicitly use folksy proverbs. Letter 19, from Wolf Wittenberg to his brother, quotes two sayings, *Oyf vos far a fur men zitst, aza nigen zingt men* . . . and *Fun shtarke tabak nist men lang* (described as a Russian proverb) and then in letter 21: "It's good in Paradise, but sins keep you out." In this context, the various Hebraisms placed in the pen of Wolf are themselves shown in a folksy light; they draw, in fact, from a popular *Yiddishkeit*—*nigen, asoro rishoynim* (itself a fairly learned expression).

Particularly prone to being germanized are the formulaic expressions that open and conclude these letters. Beginnings and endings of letters or any other type of writing are, in general, subject to maximum attention and thus tend toward fixed formulas. It is striking, in fact, that the writer(s) may opt either for Hebrew salutations (in the more intimate family letters, e.g., *ovi hayokor*), as was conventional,[29] or germanized salutations and conclusions (typically between fiancés, friends, or other nonfamily, e.g., *deine dich shatsende xxx*)— either way, there is a feel that Yiddish formulas are inadequate.

Even as one feels that the end of the letter is coming, one can detect a more formal and germanized ring. See letter 76, for example: *bei mir iz prost a yontef der tog in velchen ich derhalt fun dir a briv, un oych ven ich shreib dir a briv. Mir ducht zich az*

---

29. Compare Sholem Aleychem's *Marienbad*.

Introduction

aza ibergebene freindin vi ich bin dir hostu nit noch eyne: alzo iz mein vunsh dos undzere briv zolen nimals oyfhern. It progresses from the folksy use of words with a Hebraic and Jewish or even just a Slavic or German dialectal juice (*yontef, prost, derhaltn, ducht zich*) to the closing wish, with its germanized *dos* (for *vos*) and *nimals* (for *keynmol*). Similarly, the complimentary close: *Eier freind vos ervartet eier antvort.*

Letters of invitation and other letters of occasion seem to be particularly prone to formality, even though one might have expected that at times of birth, marriage, and so on, a more folksy and Judaic tone might surface. Thus, an invitation to a *bris* (circumcision) uses a patent Germanism: *Gestern dos morgens hot mein libe froy mir a zun geboyrn.* ("Yesterday morning my dear wife gave birth to a son"). The letter is doubly ironic, as the religious tradition is to refrain from explicitly inviting anyone to a *bris*, as the invitee is not permitted to refuse. Particularly striking is the letter of condolence with its germanized opening lines (*heite*, "today"; *erforn*, "learned"; *Ach!* instead of *Oy!*).

Sometimes Germanisms appear to be used for their comic effect: *Bester gemal* ("Dear spouse") is the highly germanized fashion in which Rosa Shochadkewitz begins her letter to her husband, describing how she just "eats and drinks and takes turns by the seashore" and asking for loads of money.

The syntax, too, is frequently germanized, with the verb being sent to the end of subordinate clauses (e.g., in the first sentence of letter 75). A formal and artificial, if not a germanized, effect is also created by the mere absence of certain words and structures and the preference for others. Thus, in relative clauses one finds *dein briv fun velchen ich ze* . . . but not *dein briv, vos ich ze fun im*—that is, the relative pronoun *velch* is employed to the exclusion of the more folksy, nonstandard German pronoun *vos*.

My translation sometimes seeks to recreate the effect. Thus, in letter 28 I have made the first sentence clumsy and used the solecism "overjoyed us" in the last sentence to recreate the stilted germanized Yiddish of a boy writing to his uncle.

To make the letters as easy as possible to read, while not detracting from the period quality, I have made them look as Yiddish as possible. I have altered germanized morphology and ignored germanized spelling—for example, *ich vinsh*, rather than *ich vinshe*; *bakumen*, rather than *bekumen*; *zun, arbet*, and *briv*, rather than *zohn, zonne, arbeit*, and *brif*—but I generally left germanized words and phrases intact, not only those grudgingly entered in Weinreich as second-rate, doubtful, or inadmissible in standard Yiddish (e.g., *tsukunftik, virklech, onkel, reize, erhalten, iberal, imer*, and *etvos*), but also those not listed at all (e.g., *fartseien, antvort, imer, nimals, zegen* ("bliss"), *leter* ("letter"!), *sheinen* ("seem"), *als* ("when"), and *tsu hoyze* . . .

Again, for the sake of easy legibility, I have transcribed the Yiddish in a slightly altered version of the standard method, with *ch* for *kh* (as in *chutspe*) and *e* inserted in words like *mazel* and *shadchen*. *Ei* represents the vowel in Einstein and *ey* the vowel in the English word prey.

BLAUSTEIN'S BRIVENSHTELER

A Letter-Writing Manual

Family Letters

1. A FATHER TO A SON

Bialistok, 10 May 1903

My dear son,

It is already some weeks that I have not received any letter from you. I am very sorry that I often have to remind you that you have a father, who wishes to know all about how you are and waits with extreme impatience for you to write. So, my dear son, have I not deserved that you should keep me in mind and grant me attention? I just cannot and will not believe that the cause of your silence is simply that all is well (knock on wood) and you don't need any favors from me. . . . So, must a father have only aggravations from children? Does a father lose his fatherly rights when one no longer needs his favor? No, my son, that is not right! You are doing wrong by not giving me, your father who loves you, the pleasure of sharing some enjoyment with a child, the perennial demand of all parents and my wish, too.

Your father,

Chaim Steinberg

On mein liben zun!

Shoyn tseit eynike vochen az ich hob fun dir keyn briv erhalten, mir tut zeyer leid vos ich darf dir oft dermonen az du host a foter, velcher vil visen ales vos mit dir iz un vart mit di greste ungeduld af dein shreiben. Shoyn zhe hob ich, mein liber zun, nit fardint bei dir du zolst mir in zinen haltn un oyfmerkzamkeyt shenken? Ich vil un ken beshum oyfen nit gloyben az di urzache fun dein shtil shveigen iz nur dos vos dir iz on ein hore gants gut un darfst nit mein laske. . . . Darf den a foter nor tsores hoben fun kinder? Farlirt den a foter dos foter-recht az men darf zein toyve nit? Neyn, mein zun, dos iz nit richtik! Du tust unrecht mit dem vos du farshafst nit mir, dein dich libenden foter, dem fargnigen a teyl tsu nemen fun naches bei a kind, vos dos iz der shtendiker farlang fun ale eltern un oych der vunsh fun mir.

Dein foter,

Chayim Shteinberg

2. REPLY

Riga, 15 May 1903

Dear beloved father,

I am in receipt of your honored missive. Your reproach is correct—I am unjust to you, dearest father! The only apology I can make is that my many affairs entail that at times I even forget about myself. However, that is hardly an excuse as far as you are concerned, and I ask of you, dear father, to forgive me this once. It shall not happen again. Writing to you will be one of my first, and most sacred, duties.

I hope that you will forgive your blameworthy son, who is devoted to you with all his heart.

Avrom Shteinberg

Teierster un fil gelibter foter!

Dein verten shreiben hob ich erhalten. Dein forvurf iz richtik—ich bin umgerecht gegen dir, bester foter! Ich ken zich farentferen nor dermit dos meine file gesheften brengen mit dos ich farges tseitenveiz vegen zich zelbst oych. Dos iz ober far dir keyn teruts nit, un ich bet dir liber foter mir dem mol antshuldiken. Dos vet mer nit farkumen. Dos shreiben tsu dir vet bei mir zein fun meine ershte un heylikste flichten.

  Ich hof az du vest fartseien dein shuldiken zun, velcher iz dir ibergeben mit dem gantsen hartsen.

Avrom Shteinberg

3. A SON TO A FATHER

Dvinsk, 2 April 1903

My dear father,

Your letter in which you write of your illness caused me great pain. Why did you not write to me about it straight away? I would forthwith have come to you so as to keep an eye on you, to get you all that was needed, and to sit by your side the whole time. I am beside myself with grief the whole day long.

Thank God, you are now improved and the doctors say that you will, please God, make a full recovery. May the Almighty grant you health and long life, so as to have joy from your children and from me, your son who treasures you.

Pinchas Gilbo

Ovi machmodi!

Dein briv, in velchen du shreibst vegen dein krankheit, hot mir fil shmertsen farshaft. Vi azoy hostu dos mir gleich nit geshriben? Ich volt umgezamt tsu dir gekumen um dir arumtsuzen, tsu shafen dir ales vos es hot zich gefordert un tsu zitsen neben dir di gantse tseit. Ich bin dem gantsen tog oyser zich fun ergernish.

A dank Got vos du bist itst beser, un di doktoyrim zogen az du vest myirtsashem fulkum gezund veren. Got zol dir shenken gezund un lange yoren, du zolst fun deine kinder naches hoben un oych fun mir dein dir shetsender zun.

Pinchas Gilbo

4. PARENTS TO A SON

Volkovishki, 6 May 1903

Our dear son Shlomo,

Your letter gave us no pleasure. Do not imagine that we expected anything other than that from you. Have we not told you all along that this would be how your searching would end? You have squandered your time and our health! What is it you were running after? Do you really lack for anything at home with your parents or do we need your earnings? We have always told you: sit at home, acquire knowledge, pay attention to the business, and get out of your head all the fantasy about earning, independence, and free living, but you've stubbornly refused to move. Well, what do you say now? It looks as if you'll be careful in future. We just wonder how you are being so foolish and still asking where you should turn and what you should do. Come home, turn to your parents, and do what they tell you. We're sending you in this letter fifteen roubles for your costs, and enough of this nonsense.

Your parents,

Azriel and Toybe Posen.

Liber zun Shloymo!

Dein briv hot undz keyn fargenigen nit farshaft. Mein nit az mir hoben fun dir vos anderes ervartet. Mir hoben doch dir ale mol gezogt az dos vet zein der sof fun deine zuchenes. Du host zich oysgebracht tseit un undz—gezunt! Noch vos bistu gelofen? Felt dir den vos in der heym bei deine eltern oder mir neytiken zich in dein fardinst? Mir hoben dir imer gezogt: zits in der heym, lern kentenishen, kuk zich tsu tsum gesheft un varf aroys fun kop di fantazye vegen fardinen, zelbshtendikeyt un frei leben, du host zich ober eingeakshent nit foren. Nu, vos zogstu yetst? Du farzogst shoyn, dacht zich, a tsenten. Undz vundert nor vi bistu azoy narish un fregst noch yetst vu du zolst zich venden un vos du zolst tun. Kum aheym, vend zich tsu deine eltern, un vos zey zogen dir dos zolstu tun. Mir shiken dir in briv fuftsen rubel af deine kosten un genug zich narish machen.

Deine eltern

Azriel *un* Toybe Pozen

5. A DAUGHTER TO A MOTHER

Odessa, 3 June 1903

Dearest Mother,

I have been meaning to write to you for some weeks now, but nothing comes of it—I am busy all the time in the house, with small children, for example, and I cannot take off any time to write. How are you, dearest mother, and how is life treating you? I just pray constantly to God that Chayele should find a good match. Then I would bring you away to me altogether. In my home you would lack nothing. I am not a lady of leisure, but, thank God, I live nicely and quietly. My husband, may he be spared, earns what we need, and I am also able to put a rouble aside. We owe no one anything, perish the thought. A beautiful house of one's own, which brings in rent, wonderful children, may they be well—and what more does a person need?

Do my brothers send you something on time every month? Do they write to you frequently? I have not had a letter from them in a long time.

Your daughter, who is always thinking of you,

Rosa Perlstein

Teierste muter!

Ich kleib zich dir shreiben shoyn fun etleche vochen, un es kumt alts nit oys—ich bin shtendik basheftikt in hoys—vi mit kleyne kinderlech, un ken zich keyn tseit nit nemen tsu shreiben. Vos machstu, libe muter, un vi lebstu? Ich bet nor shtendik Got es zol zich machen far Chayelen a guter shidech, dan volt ich dir in gantsen tsu zich tsugenumen. Bei mir volt dir fun keyn zach nit felen. Ich bin nit keyn gvirte, ober ich leb danken Got ruhik un gut. Mein man, zol leben, fardint vifil mir broychen, un ich shpar noch op a rubel; mir zeinen chas vesholem keynem nit shuldik, an eygenes hoyz a feine velche trogt dire-gelt, sheyne gerotene kinderlech zolen gezunt zein— un vos darf a mentsh noch?

Shiken dir meine brider oych pinktlech ale choydesh? Shreiben zey dir oft? Ich hob shoyn lang fun zey keyn briv nit gehat.

Dein tochter vos tracht shtendik vegen dir,

Roze Perlshtein

6. REPLY

Homel, 15 June 1903

Dear, kind daughter,

Your kind letters work the same effect on me as the best medicines. The day I get a letter from you, I feel well and refreshed. May God reward you with what you wish yourself!

I can also write you some happy news: Chayele is being proposed a really wonderful match, she's met her husband-to-be and they both like one another. When we settle the whole thing, God willing, we will invite you, meaning you with your dear husband, to the engagement (may it all work out for the best). I wrote today to the children in Boston about it. They are very prompt in sending their money. It does not go one day over, every month on the dot. May God send you, dear little children, everything you need and may I have pleasure from you all for my old age, Amen.

My warmest regards to your husband and to the dear little children. Be well and happy, all of you.

Your mother,

Chana Malkin

Libe gute tochter,

Deine gute briv virken af mir vi der bester heylmitel. Dem tog vos ich erhalt fun dir a briv bin ich gezunt un frish. Got zol dir derfar geben vos du vinsht zich aleyn!
Ich ken dir oych a freyleche neies shreiben: men ret Chayelen gor a feinem shidech, zi hot zich gezen mit dem chosen un zey gefelen zich beyde. Az mir velen myirtsashem mit ales di zach ordnen, velen mir eich, dos heyst dir mit dein liben man, af tnoim mit mazel beten. Ich hob heint vegen dem geshriben di kinder in Boston. Zey zenen zeyer pinktlech mit zeyer gelt shiken. Es geyt noch a tog nit ariber—punkt tsum choydesh. Got zol eich, libe kinderlech, alemen tsushiken ales vos ir badarft un ich zol af meine eltere yorn fun eich alemen naches hoben—omeyn.
Ich gris hertslech dein man un di kinderlach. Zeit ale gezunt un gliklech.

Eier muter,

Chane Malkin

7. A BROTHER TO A SISTER

Vitebsk, 18 July 1903

Dearest sister and brother-in-law,

    It is already two months since I wrote to you. You have no doubt been worried about my silence, for you are accustomed to receive frequent letters from me. So I am now setting your mind at rest and explaining that the cause of my not writing was my illness—for three weeks I was in bed with a very serious illness; the doctors already gave me up for lost. . . . Only God saw me through, and here you have a witness to it, that I am writing you this letter with my own hands.

    Write to me about what has happened at your end in the last few months, about your business and about everything. I'm eager to know.

Your brother,

Adolph Blumenthal

Teierste shvester un shvoger!

    Shoyn tsvey monatn iz avek zint ich hob eich geshriben. Ir zeit gevis unruik geven fun mein shtilshveigen, den ir zeit gevoynt fun mir ofte briv tsu bakumen. Alzo baruik ich eich yetst un erkler eich az di urzache fun mein nit shreiben iz geven mein krankeyt—ich bin drei vochen tsu bet gelegen in zeyer a shvere krankeyt. Di ertste hoben shoyn gehat mir antzagt. . . .

Nor Got hot mir geheylt un do hot ir a tseige, dos ich shreib eygenhendik dizen briv.

Shreibt mir vos iz bei eich forgekumen far di por monaten, fun eiere gesheftn un fun ales vos iz. Neigerik tsu visen.

Eier bruder,

Adolf Blumental

8. REPLY

Kharkov, 26 July 1903

My dear brother Adolph,

You cannot imagine how greatly your letter delighted us all. As soon as we saw the postmark "Vitebsk," our eyes lit up to read your address written in your hand. Praise be to God who saved you and raised you up from such a sickbed. Do not think, dear brother, that we knew nothing of your illness; people wrote about everything to us, once the danger was over. It has taken a heavy toll on our health, but now we're happy about your improvement. Don't strain yourself with anything, keep strictly to your diet, put everything out of your mind, and only get back to total health. I hope that we will see one another in the course of the next few weeks. . . . Be well. Your brother-in-law and sister,

Solomon and Sonia Goldfarb

Bester un teierster bruder Adolf!

Du kanst zich gor nit farshtelen vi dein briv hot undz alemen derfreit. Vi mir hoben derzen dem postshtempel "Vitebsk" iz undz lichtik gevoren in di oygen lezendik dein eygenhendike adrese. Geloybt iz Got vos hot dir geretet un oyfgehoyben fun aza bet. Meyn nit, liber bruder, az mir hoben fun dein krankeyt nit gevust. Men hot undz fun ales geshriben vi der gefar iz ariber. Es hot undz genug gezunt gekost, nor mir zeinen yetst gliklech mit dein beserung. Shtreng zich nit on mit keyn zach, hit shtreng di diete, loz ales aroys fun zinen un ver nor fulkum gezunt. Ich hof in farloyf fun eynike vochen velen mir zich zen. . . . zei gezunt vi dir vinsht dein shvoger un shvester,

Solomon *un* Sonye Goldfarb

9. A SISTER TO A BROTHER

Warsaw, 5 November 1903

Dearest brother Joseph,

From the fact that you do not write, one must conclude that you have completely forgotten about us and have no memory of your sisters and brothers. What has become of you? You used to shower us with letters and used to expect us to write to you as often as possible, and now? Now you have stopped writing altogether, stopped taking any interest in us, your sisters and brothers, for whom you take the place of a father and for whom you are the one and only comfort in hard times. . . .

Did you not promise our parents, may they rest in peace, that you, as elder brother, would care for us and be like a father? And now it is not turning out that way at all. I do not believe, I cannot and will not believe, that this is happening without a cause. My heart tells me that something unwonted has happened in your home, otherwise it would not be like this—you would not have deserted us!

So, dear brother, do not let us torment ourselves. Write us right away about how you are. As quickly as you can, reassure your worried and distressed sisters and brothers, who are beside themselves.

Your sister,

Beyle Feltenstein

Filgelibter bruder Yozef!

Vi es iz tsu shlisen fun dein nit shreiben hostu on undz gor fargesen un dermanst zich gor nit af deine shvester un brider. Vos iz dos mit dir gevoren? Du flegst doch undz farvarfen mit briv un flegst fun undz monen dir vos ofter tsu shreiben, un yetst? Yetst hostu gor oyfgehert tsu shreiben, oyfgehert tsu interesiren zich vegen undz deine shvester un brider, bei velche du bist anshtot a foter un bei velche du bist di eyntsike treyst in di shlechte tseit. . . .

Du host doch farshprochen undzere eltern aleyem-hasholem az du als elterer bruder vest far undz zorgen, vi a foter zein. Un yetst veizt dos zich gor nit aroys. Ich gloyb nit, ich ken nit un vil nit gloyben dos zol on a urzache zein. Mein harts zogt mir az es iz vos ungevoyntleches bei dir in hoyz geshen, ven nit volt azoy nit geven—du volst undz nit farlozen!

Alzo, teierer bruder, loz zich undz nit lang kvelen, shreib undz gleich vos mit dir iz. Baruik vos gicher deine unruike fartsorete shvester un brider, velche zeinen oyser zich.

Dein shvester,

Beyle Feltenshtein

10. REPLY

Minsk, 8 November 1903

Dear kind sister,

I do not have words with which to defend myself—I am truly unjust to you all. I am not only at fault to you, but have also sinned against you and against my conscience and cannot forgive myself. But you quite correctly wrote, dear sister, that there is certainly some reason for this. Yes, there was a reason, and an important one! I was burned down, had a great deal of damage and dismay, but, praise be to God—it could have been still worse. Now it is already a bit organized: I have rented a residence until I rebuild. I have been paid off fire relief and we are already half at ease.

Regarding yourselves, dear sister, I swear to you by all that is sacred that I am not forgetting you and cannot forget you. Convey this to our dear sisters and brothers from me, your brother.

Joseph Feltenstein

Libe gute shvester,

Ich hob nit keyn verter mit vos zich tsu farteydiken—ich bin virklech ungerecht gegen eich alemen. Ich bin nit nor eich shuldik nor eich zeyer zindik gegen eich un gegen mein gevisen, un ich ken zich gor nit fartseien. Du host ober richtik geshriben, libe shvester, az es iz gevis avelche urzache derbei. Yo, es iz geven a urzache un a vichtike! Ich hob opgebrent, gehat fil shoden un shrek, nor geloybt iz got derfar—es hot gekont noch erger zein. Yetst iz es shoyn abisel geordnet: Ich hob gedungen a voynung biz ich vel zich opboyen; men hot mir opgetsolt feier-kase un mir zenen shoyn halb baruikt.

Vos in eich geher, libe shvester, shver ich dir bei ales heylikes az ich farges eich nit un ken eich nit fargesen. Geb dos iber undzere libe shvester un brider in dem nomen fun mir eier bruder.

Yozef Feltenstein

Family Letters

11. A MOTHER TO A SON

Kalisch, 18 March 1903

My dear, kind son,

The news I received about you from my brother, your uncle, struck me like a thunderbolt. My child, how can you be so stupid, so thoughtless, as to throw away your studies and to let yourself into bad company?! Does it befit you, does it befit a child of respectable parents? A child whose parents are sacrificing themselves for him and trying with their last ounce of strength to educate him and make a decent individual of him? No, my son, I will not and cannot believe it! Drop this company, be obedient to your kind uncle, study diligently, and see to it that your trouble and ours does not go unvalued, and that you turn out a good person to your fellow men and to God, a credit to your loving parents.

Your mother,

Berthe Malkin

Liber guter zun meiner!

Di nachricht velche ich hob fun mein bruder dein onkl vegen dir bakumen hot mir vi a doner geshlogen. Vi kumt es tsu dir, mein kind, aza dumheyt, aza leichtzinikeyt tsu varfen dem lernen un avek lozen zich in shlechte gezelshaft?! Past es far dir, far a kind fun onshtendike eltern? Far a kind vos di eltern opferen zich far im un zeen mit di letste kraften tsu bilden im un far a mentshen tsu machen? Neyn, mein kind, ich vel nit un ken dos nit gloyben! Loz avek di gezelshaft, zei gehorchzam dein gutn onkel, lern fleisik un zey az di mi deine un undzere zol ongeleygt zein, az du zolst a mentsh veren tsu got un tsu leiten af naches far deine dir libende eltern.

Dein muter,

Berte Malkin

12. REPLY

Vilna, 23 March 1903

My dear, kind mother,

Your letter woke me as if from a slumber. I realized that I have really begun to go astray, that a young man and a child of respectable parents ought not to behave in this manner. Believe me, dear mother, it was all just a deception, a delusion to me. It was fated that you should be upset! I pledge to you, dearest mother, that from this day on I will be good and obedient, I will be rid of this whole set and will diligently get down to my studies as before, and I will be obedient to my kind uncle. I know and feel that he only has my best interests at heart and that he cares for me as for a child of his own.

Set your mind at rest, my mother! I am again, as ever before, your loving and obedient son.

Boris Malkin

Libe gute muter meine!

Dein briv hot mir vi fun shlof oyfgevekt, ich hob zich arumgezen az ich hob virklech genumen blondzhen, az nit azoy darf zich oyffiren a yunger mentsh un a kind fun sheyne eltern. Gloyb mir, libe muter, az es iz nor geven a farfirenish, a farblendenish af mir. Es iz bashert geven du zolst fardros hoben! Ich zog dir tsu, teierste muter, az ich vel fun heint on gut un gehorchzam zein, ich vel varfen di gantse gezelshaft un vel vi geven zich mit fleis far'n lernen nemen, un vel mein guten onkel gehorchzam zein, ich veys un fil az er meint nor mein toyve un az er zorgt far mir vi far an eygen kind.

Baruik zich, muter meine! Ich bin tsurik vi biz yetst dein dich libender un gehorchzamer zun.

Boris Malkin

13. A MOTHER TO A DAUGHTER

Minsk, 10 February 1903

My dear, precious daughter,

It is already fifteen years since you went away from us. In that time, much has changed. Little ones are now big ones, adults are now old, from rags to riches and from riches to rags. Much has also changed in our home—things are not what they once were! Our home no longer makes a living, it is no longer the living center it once was. It is silent—there is no sound, there is no living! . . .

The two of us, meaning myself and your old father, would have battled on as things are, for how much do we need, all told? However, we do still have a child with us, our last child and your youngest sister. She is a big girl, after all, she must have what to go out in, and it is already time to bring her to people. . . .

And so, dear daughter, we are turning to you; you are the only one in our family who can be of help in this. Take to heart your poor sister's situation, help her as far as you can, and God will help you on that account as you would wish for yourself.

Your mother who awaits your reply,

Hannah

Teiere libe tochter meine!

Es iz shoyn fariber fuftsen yor tseit du bist fun uns avek geforen. Unter der tseit hot zich fil ibergebiten: fun kleyn iz gevoren groys, fun groys—alt, fun orem—reich, un fun reich— orem. Es hot zich oych fil ibergebiten in undzer hoyz—nito vos amol iz gevezen! Undzer hoyz iz shoyn nit mer a parnose-hoys, es iz nit mer aza lebens-punkt vi geven. Es iz shtil—nito keyn geroysh, nito keyn parnose! . . .

Mir beyde, d.h. ich mit dein alten foter, volten noch vi es iz durchshlogen zich, vorem vi fil darfen mir in gantsen? Ober mir hoben doch noch bei zich a kind, undzer letste kind dein ingste shvester. Zi iz doch shoyn a groyse meydel, zi darf hoben in vos aroystsugeyn, un es iz shoyn tseit ir tsu leitn tsu brengen. . . .

Alzo, libe tochter, venden mir zich tsu dir; du bist di eyntsike in unser familye vos kenst dertsu bahilfik zein. Nem zich tsum hartsen di lage fun dein oreme shvester, helf ir vi veit du kenst un got vet dir derfar helfen vi du vinsht zich aleyn.

Dein muter vos ervartet dein entfer,

Chane

14. REPLY

New York, 15 February 1903

Dearest mother,

Your letter left a very bad impression on me. Do you really think me so bad that you write me such a pleading letter? Don't I know your situation? Don't I support you in any way possible? I have indeed written to you on several occasions that my sister should come to me in New York, that I will take her off your hands and look after her. Why on earth must you make yourself so low by writing like this? I am sending you an instruction to X office. You will receive the money there right away. See to get an outfit for my sister to come to me in, and rely on me—she will have everything she needs.

Your daughter,

Lena Bernstein

Teierste muter!

Dein briv hot af mir zeyer a shlechten eindruk gemacht. Haltst du mir den azoy shlecht az du shreibst mir aza tachnunimdiken briv? Veys ich den nit eier tsustand? Shtits ich eich nit vi nor miglech iz? Ich hob doch eich eynike mol geshriben az mein shvester zol tsu mir noch Nyu York kumen, az ich nem ir op fun eich un vel far ir zorgen? Vos zhe darfstu azoy niderik machen zich mit dein shreiben? Ich shik dir an onveizung in n.n. kantor, du vest dorten gleich dos gelt bakumen. Ze af mein shvester a kostyum, in velchen zi zol kenen tsu mir kumen, un farloz zich af mir—es vet ir nit felen keyn zach.

Dein tochter,

Lina Berenshtein

15. A FATHER TO A SON

New York, 9 January 1903

My dear, faithful son,

I have been meaning to send you this letter for a long while, but it has been hard for me to do it. I cannot wait any longer now, and I am writing regardless. You have quite forgotten your old father, although your old father has no one beside you who can help him in his need. You have forgotten that your father, who cared for you more than for his own self, is old and poor and has to depend on you to keep him going. You forget that old folk, as long as they are alive, wish to eat precisely like young people. . . . Had you not forgotten this, you would surely have written sometime or other to your old father and supported him as far as you could.

It is no good when one has to depend on strangers, but it is still worse when children on whom one has to depend turn their back on their parents. . . . I have already sold everything off just in order not to be dependent on anyone; now, though, I no longer have what to sell.

Think, my son, of the plight of your poor, old father, who is lonely besides.

Azriel Posen

Guter treier zun meiner!

Ich hob dir shoyn lang dizen briv gevolt shreiben, es iz mir ober shver geven. Yetst ken ich shoyn mer nit varten un shreib doch. Du host zich gor on dein alten foter fargesen, obvol dein alter foter hot oyser dir keynem nit ver es zol im bahelfik zein in zein noyt. Du host fargesen az der foter deiner, velcher hot far dir mer vi far zich gezorgt, iz alt un orem un muz onkumen tsu dir um zein leben tsu derhalten. Du fargest az alte mentshen kol zman zey leben vilen zey esen punkt vi yunge. . . . Ven du volst dos nit fargesen volstu doch ven dein alten foter geshriben un geshtitst im vi veit dein miglechkeyt iz.

Es iz nit gut ven men darf onkumen tsu fremde, es iz ober noch erger az kinder tsu velche men darf onkumen farfremden zich fun zeyere eltern. . . . Ich hob shoyn ales oysfarkoyft nor tsu keynem nit ontsukumen, ich hob ober mer nit vos tsu farkoyfen.

Batracht, mein zun, di lage fun mir dein altn oremen foter, vos iz dertsu noch elent oych.

Azriel Pozen

16. REPLY

Chicago, 15 January 1903

My dearly beloved father,

    I am beside myself with your letter, from which I see how badly off you are, and even more so with the fact that you have a complaint against me. I am wrong to write to you so seldom, although I am always preoccupied with business, which is not going too well, as with everyone recently. This much is correct; but can you really blame me for not supporting you, when you have never written to me that you lack anything? Am I a prophet? Can I, living in Chicago, know that you, dear father, are suffering hardship in New York? Now that I know, I am sending you fifty dollars right away and promise to send you support every month, so that you should lack for nothing, Heaven forbid. And you should not deny yourself, dear father—eat and drink to your heart's content.

Your son,

Shlomo Posen

Ovi yakiri umachmodi!

    Ich bin oyser zich fun dein briv fun velchen ich ze vi shlecht dir iz, un noch mer fun dem vos du host a pretenzye tsu mir. Ich hob umrecht vos ich shreib tsu dir zeyer zelten, obvol ich bin shtendik fardret in gesheft, velcher get, vi alemen di letste tseit, nit am besten. Dos iz richtik; ober kenstu mir den bashuldiken far vos ich shtits dir nit, az du host mir keyn mol nit geshriben az dir felt? Bin ich den a novi? Ken ich voynendik in Shikago visen az du, liber foter, leidst noyt in Nyu York? Yetst az ich veys shik ich dir gleich fuftsik doler, un zog dir tsu monatlech shtitse tsu shiken um dir zol chas vesholem gor nit felen. Un du, liber foter, zolst nit kargen—es un trink vos dein harts gelust.

Dein zun,

Shloyme Pozen

17. ONE BROTHER TO ANOTHER

Grodno, 19 May 1903

Dearest brother,

It has been a long time since we stopped corresponding. I do not know the cause and I believe that you likewise do not know either—it kind of came about for no good reason! But it is hardly proper for the two of us; two brothers ought not to act in this way when they are just the two and have no other family. This is not how it should be! So I am asking you, dear brother, write to me about how you are, how is life in America? What business are you in? What children do you have, whether you are happy with America, these are all things that I am very curious to know.

I hope that from now on we will correspond frequently and without a break. Your brother,

Wolf Wittenberg

Teierster bruder!

Es iz shoyn a lange tseit fariber zint mir hoben oyfgehert durchshreiben zich. Di urzache derfun veys ich nit un gloyb az du dos gleichen veyst oych nit—dos iz epes stam azoy gevoren! Doch iz dos nit orntlech fun undz beyden, nit azoy darfen ton tsvey brider, velche zenen nor tsvey un hoben mer in familye keynem nit, es darf azoy nit zein! Alzo bet ich dir, liber bruder, shreib mir vos mit dir iz, vi lebstu in Amerika? Vos iz dein gesheft? Vos hostu far kinderlech un oyb du bist mit Amerika tsufriden, ich bin dos ales zeyer neigerik tsu visen.

Ich farhof az fun yetst velen mir zich korespondiren oft un on oyfher. Dein bruder,

Volf Vitenberg

18. REPLY

New York, 5 June 1903

Dear brother Wolf,

I received your letter correctly, although I have already switched apartments three times after my old address. The mail here is functioning well—no letters go astray and they track down the addressee.

I cannot put into words what pleasure your letter gave me. You are right, dear brother, this is not how it ought to be, but surely you know that "things are not always how they ought to be" . . . I imagine that you feel this way at your end quite often, a lot of things over there ought not to be as they are and really aren't what they should be. . . .

Here I make a living; you can here—no one bothers you. Everyone can earn his money at whatever he wants, and wherever he wishes. So you can appreciate that my line of business is something that suits me and is most worthwhile. I have three lovely daughters and two sons, who are getting their education free of charge in the best schools, together with all children—so what do you say, ought I not to be happy with America?

Tell me how things are with you there. A letter from you will bring joy to the whole of your brother's family.

Solomon Wittenberg

Liber bruder Volf!

Dein leter hob ich richtik erhalten, obvol ich hob shoyn drei voynungen gebiten noch mein alten adres. Bei undz iz in post zeyer gute ordnung—keyn briv geyt nit farfalen un men zucht af dem adresat.

Dem fargenigen vos dein briv hot mir farshaft bin ich nit in shtand dir oystsushreiben. Du host recht, guter bruder, es darf azoy nit zein, nor veystu den nit az "nit ales iz vi es darf zein." . . . Mir dacht az bei eich filt ir dos gants oft, fil zachen hot bei eich gedarft zein nit vi es iz un es iz doch nit vi es darf. . . .

Ich mach do a leben; do ken men a leben machen—men shtert nit; yeder ken zich fardinen fun vos er vil un vu er vil. Alzo kenstu farshteyn az mein gesheft iz vos mir past un vos mir iz leyniger. Ich farmeg drei sheyne techter un tsvey zin, velche bakumen bildung umzist in di beste shulen mit ale kinder tsu gleich—nu, zol ich mit Amerika nit tsufriden zein?!

Shreib mir vos iz dorten mit dir, du vest mit dein shreiben erfreien di gantse familye fun dein bruder.

Zalamon Vitenberg

19. WOLF TO SOLOMON

Grodno, 20 June 1903

Dearest brother Solomon,

My wish has indeed been granted—I have at last received a letter from you, and, thank God, a very happy one. I must tell you quite frankly, brother, that I cannot write such good things about myself. But I do not want you to think I am an exception! I don't think that here in our part of the world there is a Jew who makes a decent living. We all live off air, and I daresay in misery, too. From your letter I understand that you know about our life, although you have been eighteen years in America. "If the tobacco is strong, the cough will be long," says a Russian proverb. But what can we do!?

I have two sons and one daughter. I am not educating my sons, because education in the home costs a lot and it is very difficult to get into a school—after all, not everyone can be the first in line. . . . So, things are indeed dire—we cannot even derive much joy from the children, although they are bright.

Forgive me, my dear brother, for singing such a lonesome song—"You sing the song of the wagon you're on . . ."

All the best to your wife and children. My wife and children send you warmest regards.

Your brother,

Wolf Wittenberg

Teierste bruder Zalamon!

Mein vunsh iz doch erfilt gevoren—ich hob fun dir endlech a briv bakumen, un danken Got zeyer a freilechen. Ich muz dir ofen shreiben, bruder, az ich ken dir fun zich azoy gut nit shreiben. Nor meyn nit az ich bin an oysname! Mir ducht az do bei unz macht keyn yid keyn leben nit. Mir leben ale fun vind un efsher oych mit vind. Fun dein briv iz tsu farshteyn az du veyst fun undzer leben chotsh du bist in Amerika shoyn tseit achtsen yor. "Fun shtarke tabak nist men lang" zogt a rusisher shprichvort, vos kenen mir ober tun!?

Ich hob tsvey zin un eyn tochter. Meine zin bilde ich nit, vayl hoyz-bildung kost teier un in a shule iz zeyer shver areintsugeyn, nit ale kenen doch zein fun di asoro rishoynim. . . . Alzo iz take zeyer biter—mir kenen amol keyn naches fun kinder oych nit hoben, obvoyl zey zenen feyike.

Antshuldik, liber bruder, vos ich zing mit azoy an umediken nigen—"oyf vos far a fur men zitst, aza nigen zingt men . . ."

Gris in mein nomen dein froy un kinder. Mein froy un di kinder grisen aych zeyer.

Dein bruder,

Volf Vitenberg

20. SOLOMON TO WOLF

New York, 8 July 1903

You need not ask for my indulgence, dear brother, for your lonesome song; I was expecting it—I knew it in advance! It surprises you that in the course of eighteen years I have not forgotten about Jewish life or about your sweat and toil; some surprise! It would have been far more surprising if I had forgotten it in eighteen years; in fact, I do not think that anyone could forget it. . . .

If it is still possible, follow me, dear brother, sell everything you have; turn it all into cash and come out to us. In our part of the world, everyone is free to come at any time. Here you will know the meaning of earning a living; here you will be able to make a *mentsh* of your children and live like a *mentsh*. . . . Come over, my brother, and the two of us will no longer be lonely.

Write straight away to me about how you see this, as I await your reply with the utmost impatience.

Your brother,

Solomon Wittenberg

Du farshporst, liber bruder, tsu beten bei mir antshuldikung far dein umediken lid; ich hob es ervartet—ich hob es faroys gevust! Dir vundert dos ich hob in farloyf fun achtsen yor nit fargesen vegen dem yidishen leben, oder mutshen zich bei eich; es iz keyn vunder! Es volt fil mer geven vos tsu bavunderen ven ich volt dos fargesen in achtsen yor, mir ducht az in achtsen yor ken men dos oych nit fargesen. . . .

Oyb es iz nor meglech, folg mir, liber bruder, farkoyf als vos du host; mach als tsu gelt un kum tsu undz, bei undz iz frei alemen un ale mol tsu kumen. Do vestu fun a leben visen, do vestu kenen deine kinder far mentshen machen un leben vi a mentsh . . . Kum, mein bruder, mir velen beide nit mer elent zein.

Shreib mir gleich dein meinung vegen dem. Den oyf dein antvort vart mit dem gresten ungedult.

Dein bruder,

Zalamon Vitenberg

21. WOLF TO SOLOMON

Grodno, 25 July 1903

My dear brother Solomon,

"It's good in Paradise, but sins keep you out"—this saying occurred to me. Reading your sweet words, I feel like getting up and coming your way immediately, to the latterday Land of Israel, to the place where you can earn money by your efforts, where work is rewarded, and where every human being can engage in whatever he wishes and wherever he so wishes—but such a trip takes money; and the only money I can make is from my house, if I were to sell it. But there are no dealers now, no one wants to put money into a house. Everyone would rather be a rich tenant than a poor homeowner. So, what can one do?

And so, dear brother, one will have to go on being patient. Maybe the bad situation will improve with time, and then I will do your asking and my desire. . . .

Your brother,

Wolf Wittenberg

Teierster guter bruder Zalamon!

"Es iz gut in Gan-Eyden, ober di zind lozen nit arein"—der shprichvort iz oysgekumen oyf mir. Lezendik deine zise verter vilt zich gleich nemen un furen tsu dir, in dem heintiken Erets-Yisroel, in dem ort vu men ken mit mi fardinen, vu arbet vert batsolt un vu yeder mentsh ken zich basheftiken mit vos er vil un vu er vil—ober tsu aza reize fodert zich gelt; un gelt machen ken ich nor fun mein hoyz ven ikh zol ir farkoyfen, es iz ober yetst keyn sochrim nito, keyner vil nit areinlegen keyn gelt in a hoyz. Yeder vil beser zein a reicher shochen eyder an oremer balabos. Nu, vos ken men tun?

Alzo, liber bruder, muz dos noch geduldik zein. Mit der tseit vet zich fileicht osybeseren der shlechter tsushtand un dan vel ich tun dein farlang un mein vunsh. . . .

Dein bruder,

Volf Vitenberg

22. SOLOMON TO WOLF

New York, 12 August 1903

Dearest brother Wolf,

I do not understand you—whether or not you are right to torment yourself and suffer while you wait for better times, you certainly have no right to torture your young children, who will come to nothing there with you and who will blame you as long as they live for forcing them to remain in their awful circumstances; this is something that you must not and may not do! Do not wait for better times, your waiting will get you nowhere! Go ahead and get yourself packed up, cut loose from everything, and come out to us without delay. A hundred rubles more or less is nothing; life is more precious!

I am sure that you will do what I am advising you and see no need to write a whole deal about it.

Your brother,

Solomon Wittenberg

Teierster bruder Volf!

Ich farshtey dir nit—oyb du host recht zich tsu kvelen un leiden zelbst vartendik oyf beser, ober tsu mutshen deine yunge kinder, fun velche dorten bei dir vet gor nisht veren un velche velen tseit zeyer leben baklogen zich oyf dir vos du host zey geneyt in zeyer shlechten tsushtand tsu bleiben—hostu gevis keyn recht nit; du darfst dos nit tun un torst dos nit tun! Vart nit oyf beser, es iz umzist dayn varten! Nem un pekel zich tsuzamen, shneid op fun als un kum umgezamt tsu undz. Hundert rubel mer oder veyniker iz gor nisht; der leben iz teierer!

Ich bin zicher az du vest tun vos ich rate dir un gefin nit far neytik fil vegen dem tsu shreiben.

Dein bruder,

Zalomon Vitenberg

23. ONE BROTHER TO ANOTHER

Hudson, 5 October 1903

My dear brother,

I just cannot imagine what to make of your silence. I have already written three letters to you and have not received a reply. Write me how you are, as I am very worried.

Your brother,

Zusmann Finkelstein

Ochi hayokor!

Ich ken gor nit klug veren vos dein shtilshveigen zol badeiten, ich hob dir shoyn drei briv geshriben un hob fun dir keyn entfer nit erhalten.
Shreib mir vos iz mit dir, den ich bin zeyer unruik.

Dein bruder,

Zusman Finklshtein

24. REPLY[30]

Mitava, 9 October 1903

Dearest brother,

Forgive me for not having written to you in so long, but, unfortunately, I have not been able to write. The reason for this is that I have no good news to write to you, and to apprise you of my shabby life, of my destitution and troubles, is something I simply did not wish to do. I appreciate that you will derive no pleasure from this. . . .

Some years ago when I received residency rights in Courland, I felt ecstatic, but it was an empty fantasy. Now, everywhere they have set up cooperative stores which are in competition with Jewish businesses; many lines of business are entirely prohibited to Jews and expenses are high. . . .

This is the only reason that I did not write to you until you wrote to me about being worried for me.

Your brother,

Leon Finkelstein

---

30. I have used a more formal English to match the germanized grammar. The correspondent is writing from Courland (in modern-day Latvia), a particularly germanized region, and the *Brivenshteler* has skillfully adjusted the style accordingly.

Teierster bruder!

Antshuldik mir vos ich hob dir azoy lang nit geshriben, ich hob ober leider nit gekent shreiben. Di urzache derfun iz dos vos ich hob keyne gute neies dir tsu shreiben, un mitteylen dir fun mein gemein leben, fun mein armut un tsores hob ich poshet nit gevolt. Ich farshtey az du vest fun dem keyn fargenigen hoben. . . .

Mit a por yor tsurik az ich hob bakumen voynrecht in kurland hob ich gemeynt az ich bin ibergliklech, es iz ober geven a piste fantazye. Iberal zeinen yetst gefunt gevoren gezelshafts-kromen, velche farkonkuriren di idishe gesheftn; fil gesheftn zeinen in gantsen far iden farboten un di hoytsoe is groys. . . .

Ot dos iz di eyntsike urzache vos ich hob dir nit geshriben, biz du host mir vegen dein baumruiken zich iber mir geshriben.

Dein bruder,

Leon Finkelshtein

25. SHIMON TO BORUCH

Pinsk, 19 September 1903

Dear brother,

Your letter gave us great pleasure. Thank God, you are well and business is going well. In these times, that is a rarity. I wish always to receive letters like this from you.

About myself, I do not really have any good news to write, unfortunately. Business is shrinking by the year, the family is growing, and the expenses are unbearable. I just live, like all Jews, in the hope that things will become better, God willing—to hope, after all, costs nothing. . . .

Your brother,

Shimon Lioznov

Ochi yokor venechmod!

Dein briv hot undz fil fargenigen farshaft. Danken Got far dein gezunt un vos du machst gute gesheften, bei di yetstike tseit iz dos a zeltenheyt. Ich vinsh imer fun dir azelche briv tsu bakumen.

Fun zich ken ich dir leider keyn tsu gute neies nit shreiben. Di gesheften veren fun yor klener, di familye greser un di hoytsoe iz nit tsu dertrogen. Nor vi ale iden leb ich in hofnung az es vet im yirtse hashem beser veren—hofen kost doch keyn gelt nit. . . .

Dein bruder,

Shimen Lioznov

26. REPLY

Tshernigov, 27 September 1903

Dear brother Shimon,

Reading your letter, it occurred to me to suggest to you that you might wish to lighten your expenses and send your elder son to me. I have a vacancy here for a bookkeeper. I know, of course, that your children are well-educated, capable, and organized to the nth degree—it will be good for both of us: I will have a bookkeeper whom I can trust like my own self, and he will have a position with me, his uncle, who knows how to appreciate him. Besides that, the position will give him a nice salary.

I await your reply via your son!

Your brother,

Boruch Lioznov

Teyerster bruder Shimen!

Lezendik dein briv iz mir eingefalen dir fortsuleygen fileicht vestu velen fargringeren zich di oysgaben (hoytsoe) un vest tsu mir dein eltern zun shiken. Bei mir iz yetst do a vakansie oyf a shtele far a buchhalter. Ich ken doch deine kinder dos zey zenen gebildete, feike un oyf'n hechsten fal ordentliche—es vet far undz beyde gut zein: ich vel hoben a buchhalter, oyf velchen ich vel zich kenen farlozen vi oyf zich zelbst; un er vet hoben a shtele

bei mir, zein onkel, vos veys vi im tsu shatsen. Oyser vos di shtele vet im sheyne gehalt trogen.
   Ich vart oyf dein antvort durch dein zun!

Dein bruder,

Boruch Lioznov

27. SHIMON TO BORUCH

Pinsk, 6 October 1903

I cannot begin to thank you as you deserve. Your letter gladdened us all. You do indeed have a large business, my son will gain some good experience, and we hope that you will both be extraordinarily satisfied.

Your wish, kind brother, for my reply to be sent to you via my son, your future bookkeeper, is one that I cannot fulfill—a few more days must elapse until he can travel. I am clothing him as befits a bookkeeper of yours and as is proper for arriving in a large city. My son is writing you a letter of his own today or tomorrow.

Your brother,

Shimon Lioznov

Ich bin nit in shtand dir noch dein vert tsu badanken. Dein briv hot undz alemen derfreit: Bei dir iz doch a groyser gesheft, mein zun vet gute praktike hoben, un mir hofen az ir vet beyde hechst tsufriden zein.

Dein vunsh, guter bruder, tsu shiken dir mein antvort durch mein zun, dein tsukunftiken buchhalter, ken ich nit erfilen—es muz noch eynike teg gedoyren biz er vet kenen foren. Ich bakleyd im vi es past far dein a buchhalter un vi es iz onshtendik in a groyse shtot tsu kumen. Mein zun shreibt dir bazunder a briv heint oder morgen.

Dein bruder,

Shimen Lioznov

28. A NEPHEW TO AN UNCLE[31]

Pinsk, 8 October 1903

Most esteemed Uncle,

I am writing you a short letter, as I am so surprised by my good fortune in being written to by you that I cannot gather my thoughts. I cannot even thank you at this moment as befits you—that is something I will do in person in a few days, when I come to see you. There is only one thing that I can write to you: You have overjoyed us all!

Your nephew who wishes you well,

Jacob Lioznov

Geertester onkel, lebt voyl!

Ich shreib eich a kurtsen briv, den ich bin zo iberrasht fun eier far mir gliklechen shreiben dos ich ken meine gedanken nit tsuzamen nemen. Ich ken eich zogar yetst nit danken noch eier vert—dos vel ich mindlech machen in farloyf fun eynike teg, ven ich vel tsu eich kumen. Eyn zach ken ich eich nor shreiben: Ir hot undz alemen ibergliklech gemacht!

Eier eich glikvinshender plimenik,

Yakob Lioznov

---

31. I have made the first sentence clumsy and used the solecism "overjoyed us" in the last sentence to recreate the stilted germanized word order and vocabulary of a boy writing to his uncle.

29. ONE SISTER TO ANOTHER

Yekaterinoslav, 5 April 1903

My dear sister Lina,

Last week I had regards from you via Miss _____. She told me that life is going quite well for you and you are content. I was very happy to hear that, and I pray to God that things should always go well and happily for you!

I am living here all alone. Here in Yekaterinoslav no one has much of a life; from morning to night people wear themselves out earning their crust of bread. Write to me whether I could make something of my laundry concern in your part of the world in Libava.[32] I have studied the trade thoroughly. Here, unfortunately, it can only bring me in a tiny income.

If this is a good idea, write to me and I will come out to you. There I will earn a living and not be lonely.

Your sister,

Rose Rosenzweig

---

32. In modern-day Latvia.

Teierste shvester Lina!

Di forike voch hob ich fun dir durch freilein _____ a grus gehat. Zi hot mir gezogt az dir lebt zich gants gut un lebst in tsufridenheyt. Dos hot mir zeyer gefreyt. Gib Got es zol dir imer freylech un gut zein!

Ich leb do gants eynzam. Bei undz in Yekaterinoslav veys keyner nit fun a leben; men iz fun morgen biz ovent farhorevet in fardinen dos shtikel broyt. Shreib mir oyb ich volt kenen vos machen mit mein vesh-geyn bei eich in Libava. Ich hob di arbet grindlech erlernt. Do, leyder, ken es mir gor veynik fardinst brengen.

Oyb dos iz a plan shreib mir, vel ich ariberforen tsu dir. Dorten vel ich fardinen un vel nit elent zein.

Dein shvester,

Roze Rozentsveig

30. REPLY

Libava, 10 April 1903

Dear sister Rose,

I have received your letter. I conferred with my husband and he is also of the opinion that you can make a good living here from your work. So write to us whether you are thoroughly skilled in the job, whether you have a testimonial from a firm that you worked for, and whether you are in a position to run a modern workshop. There is no joy to be had from using your own ten fingers. But if you open a workshop, we hope you will earn good money—you will have no shortage of customers.

Your sister,

Lina Rosenbaum

Teierste shvester Roze!

Dein briv hob ich erhalten. Ich hob zich baraten mit mein liber man, er iz oych in dem meinung az du kenst do fun dein arbet gut fardinen. Alzo shreib undz oyb du bist folkom ferem in di arbet, oyb du host an atestat fun a firme, far velche du host gearbet un oyb du bist im shtande tsu firen a moderne verkhoyz. Fun di eygene tsen finger ken men keyn gliken nit onleben. Ven du zolst ober a verk-hoyz efenen, hofen mir az du vest gut fardinen—keyn kundshaft vet dir nit felen.

Dein shvester,

Lina Rozenboym

31. ROSE TO LINA

Yekaterinoslav, 15 April 1903

Dear sister and brother-in-law, may fortune smile on you,

It makes me so happy that I am able to write back in agreement with you on all your questions: I have a testimonial from a certain local ready-to-use laundry firm, M. Atzarkin and Co., in which they state clearly that I know the job thoroughly, that I worked for them for three years as a supervisor and manager of workshops, in which there were always fifteen to twenty seamstresses at work.

And so, my dear, you have "one" answer to "all" your questions. I believe the answer is just as you desired. In order that you should be able to speak about my work with acquaintances of yours, I am enclosing my testimonial with this letter.

Your sister,

Rose Rosenzweig

Teierste shvester un shvoger lebt gliklech!

Ich ken eich tsu mein groysen fargenigen oyf ale eiere fragen einshtimik antvorten: Ich hob an atestat fun a hizike gevise firme fun fartike veshe, M Atsarkin et kop, in velche zey hobn deitlech geshriben dos ich ken di artbet grindlech, dos ich hob bei zey gearbet drei yor als oyfpaserin un firerin fun masterskaye, in velche es hoben shtendik gearbet 15-20 neyterins.

Alzo, meine teierste, hot ir "eyn" antvort oyf "ale" eiere fragen. Ich gloyb der antvort iz vi gevunshen far eich. Um ir zolt kenen vegen mein arbet mit bakante mentshen reden, shik ich eich bei dizen briv mein atestat.

Eier shvester,

Roze Rozentsveig

32. LINA TO ROSE

Libava, 23 April 1903

Dear Rose,

We have already spoken to some rich households about you. We have also shown them your testimonial. They all say the same thing, that you can do good business here.

So, dear sister, put everything straight so as to be able to come out to us as quickly as possible. The summer season is beginning now, as well as the *dacha* season. Now is the time to make a good start. Write to us the exact day of your arrival and we will wait for you at the station.

Your sister,

Lina Rosenbaum

Teierste Roze!

Mir hoben shoyn geret mit eynige reiche heizer vegen dir. Oych hoben mir zey gevizen dein atestat. Ale zogen dos zelbike, az du kenst do gute gesheft machen.

Alzo, teierste shvester, mach als in ordnung um du zolst vos shneler kenen tsu undz kumen. Der zumer sezon heybt zich yetst on, oykh der datshes sezon. Yetst kenstu a guten anfang machen. Shreib undz bashtimt dem tog fun dein kumen, velen mir dir oyf dem ban ervarten.

Dein shvester,

Lina Rozenboym

33. A SISTER TO A BROTHER

Kursk, 10 May 1903

Dearest brother,

I am writing to inform you that my wish has been fulfilled—I am engaged to Max Beierfeld, to whom my parents and I have taken a great liking and of whom everyone speaks highly. This is the good news that we promised to write to you in our previous letter.
I am happy and I wish you the same!

Your sister,

Helena

Teierster un liber bruder!

Ich kum dir mittsuteylen dos mein vunsh iz erfilt gevoren— ich bin farlobt (tnoim gemacht) mit Maks Beierfeld, velcher iz meine eltern un mir zeyer gefelen un fun alemen zeyer gerimt. Dos iz di gute neies, velche mir hoben dir in undzer foriken briv tsugezogt tsu shreiben.
Ich bin gkiklech un vinsh dos oych dir!

Dein shvester,

Helena

34. REPLY

Berditchev, 8 May 1903

Dear sister Helena,

I congratulate you and wish you the same happiness that you and your cherished husband-to-be would wish yourselves. Please God that you may both always be content and live in prosperity and peace.

It may be that I will shortly also be able to write you such news. . . . Give my best wishes, sight unseen, to your fiancé, and tell him that he is already the subject of his future brother-in-law's esteem.

Yitschok

Libe shvester Helena!

Ich gratulir dir un vinsh dir glik vi du un dein geshatster broytigam (chosen) vinsht zich zelbst. Gib Got ir zolt imer tsufriden zein beyde un leben in guts un friden!
Es ken zein az kirtslech vel ich eich oych aza neies shreiben kenen. . . . Gris unbekanterveiz dein broytigam fun meint vegen, un zog im dos es shatst im shoyn zein tsukinftiker shvoger.

Yitschok

35. MAX TO YITZCHOK

Kursk, 27 May 1903

My highly esteemed future brother-in-law,

We have duly received your letter of congratulation. Many thanks from my dear bride and myself for your warm, brotherly letter. Please God that your wish for us be fulfilled and equally our wishes for your own happiness.
I hope, dear brother, that we will shortly make each other's acquaintance and that we will then remain brothers for ever.

Wishing you every happiness,

Max Beierfeld

Hoychgeshatster tsukunftiker shvoger!

Eier gratulatsionsbriv (glikvinshenden) hoben mir richtik erhalten. Ich un mein libe broyte (kale) danken eich fil mol far eier bruder-freintlechen briv. Gib Got eier vunsh af undz zol erfilt veren vi oych undzer glikvinshen eich.
Ich hof, liber bruder, az mir velen zich kirtslech kenen lernen un dan velen mir af eybik brider bleiben.

Eier eich glikvinshender,

Maks Beierfeld

36. REPLY

Berditchev, 7 June 1903

Brother Max,

You write that after I come and we get to know each other personally, we will remain brothers for life. I see it differently—from the moment you became my dear sister's fiancé, we were already brothers.

I am sending you this letter to my sister's address. I believe you will receive it promptly. Send regards in my name to your fiancée and tell her that I will forthwith thoroughly discuss everything with her personally and verbally.

Your brother,

Yitschok

Bruder Maks!

Du shreibst az nochdem az ich vel kumen un mir velen zich perzenlech bakenen, velen mir brider tseit undzer leben bleiben; ich mein andersh—mir zeinen shoyn brider koym bistu mein shvesters broytigam.

Ich shik dir dem briv af mein shvesters adrese. Ich gloyb du vest im pinktlech bakumen. Gris in mein nomen dein broyte un zog ir az ungezamt vel ich zich mit ir perzenlech un mindlech iber ales oysreden.

Eier bruder,

Yitschok

Love Letters

37. PHILLIP TO ANNA

Bialistok, 1 April 1903

Worthy Miss Anna Scheinfinkel,

I take a hazardous step, but "If one takes no risks," as the proverb goes, "one does not win the bout." So I am daring to do it.

I mean to say that you must have noticed that I am not indifferent to you, that I am an entirely different person in your company, and, indeed, that the relationship has made a great impression upon me. . . .

I cannot for long remain in the circumstances in which I now find myself; that would be an impossibility! I am therefore asking you, treasured Anna, to make me happy with a single word of yours. With a single word of yours, you can either put me completely at ease and make me happy forever, or, quite the contrary . . . The choice is yours, and my life, my peace of mind, and happiness are suspended from your word. . . .

I await your reply with the greatest impatience,

Phillip Eichhorn

Vertes froylein Ana Sheynfinkl!

Ich mach yetst a geferlechen shrit, nor "ver es shtelt zech nit in gefar," zogt a shprichvort, "gevint nit di shtreit," alzo vage ich ich es tsu ton.

Ich meyn dos ir hot bamerkt az ich bin tsu eich nit gleichgiltik, az in eier gezelshaft bin ich gor an ander mentsh un oych dos az di farheltnis hot af mir zeyer a groysen eindruk gemacht. . . .

In dem tsushtand vu ich bin yetst ken ich lang nit bleiben, dis iz an unmegleche zach! Alzo bet ich eich, hochgeshetste Anna, mir mit eier eyn vort gliklech tsu machen, mit eier eyn vort kent ir mir oder in gantsen baruiken un af eyvik gliklech machen, oder in gegenteyl . . . Der val iz tsu eich, un mein leben, mein baruigung un glik hengen af eier vort. . . .

Ich ervarte mit dem gresten ungeduld eier antvort.

Filip Eichhorn

38. ANNA TO PHILLIP

Grodno, 4 April 1903

Most honored Mr. Eichhorn,

Although your letter made me proud and your heartfelt words flattered my self-esteem exceedingly, I find that I myself have no right to give my hand, even to a person such as you, before telling my dear parents about it and listening to their views.
For my part I can write to you that I esteem you as fully befits you, that your company has the same effect on me as you wrote of to me. . . . But, in my case, it happens that parents deserve not to be dispensed with for such a step as this.
That, for the time being, is my answer, which I fancy will give you some little peace of mind. I would appreciate your views concerning the contents of this letter.

Respectfully,

Anna Scheinfinkel

Geertester her Eichhorn,

Obvol eier briv hot mir shtolts gemacht un eier tif fun hartsen geredte verter hoben mein eygenlibe zeyer geshmeichelt, doch gefin ich dos ich zelbst hob keyn recht mein hand tsu geben, zogar aza perzon vi ir, eyder ich vel meine libe eltern vegen dem zogen, un zeyer meinung oysheren.

Fun meiner zeite ken ich eich shreiben dos ich shets eich noch eier vert, dos eier gezelshaft macht af mir dem zelbiken virkung vi ir hot mir geshriben. . . . Nor bei mir kumt oys az eltern fardinen dos bei aza shrit zol men zich on zey nit bageyn.

Dos iz farloyfik mein antvort, velcher ich rechn vet eich a bisl baruiken. Ich vinsh eier meinung tsu bakumen vegen dem inhalt fun mein dizen briv.

Mit achtung,

Ana Sheynfinkl

39. PHILLIP TO ANNA

Bialistok, 6 April 1903

Worthy Miss Scheinfinkel,

To you my writing may have brought pride, to you my words may have been pleasing, but to me your letter has given the gift of life and eternal bliss! I have read your letter between the lines and found there more than is written. . . . I already have a happy beginning—I already have something for which to hope. Now I feel the thrust of the proverb: "What is lacking in the here and now, hope makes up for with the future." Ah! Dear hope and sweet future! You now take up a great part of my life. . . .

I am wholly in agreement with your opinion. Parents deserve it that children, from whom they suffer so much until one has brought them up, should ask their opinion on such a step. But I do not have patience enough to await their happy acquiescence.

Your Phillip Eichhorn

Vertes froylein Sheynfinkl!

Eich hot mein shreiben shtolts gemacht, eich hoben meine verter geshmeychelt; mir ober hot eier briv dem leben geshonken un af eybik gliklech gemacht! Ich hob in eier briv geleynt tsvishn di reyen (shures). Ich hob in im gefunen mer vi es iz in im geshriben. . . . Ich hob shoyn a gliklechen onfang—ich hob shoyn af vos tsu hofen. Yetst fil ich dem gedrang fun folks-vertel: "Vos es felt in yetst, derleygt di hofnung mit dem tsukunft." Ah! Libe hofnung un ziser tsukunft! Ir farnemt bei mir yetst a groysen teyl in mein leben. . . .

Mit eier meynung bin ich fulkum eynshtimik. Eltern zeinen vert az kinder, fun velche zey leiden zo fil biz men ertsit zey, zolen bei aza shrit zeyer meynung fregen. Ich hob ober nit azoy fil geduld zeyer gliklechen eynshtimung tsu dervarten.

Eier Filip Eichhorn

40. ANNA TO PHILLIP

Grodno, 12 April 1903

Most honored Phillip,

Your last letter is a mirror of my feelings, the words are almost taken from my mouth, my life is now accompanied by those same two angels, hope and future. I am just not so brazen as to suggest such a thing to my good parents—this is too difficult an undertaking for a woman. Advise me how it should happen, I cannot do it, it is costing me my health and costing you your patience.

Your Anna Scheinfinkel

Geertester Filip!

In eier letstn briv zeinen opgeshpigelt meine gefilen, di verter zeinen vi fun mein mund aroysgenumen, mein leben bagleiten yetst oych di zelbike tsvey englen (malochim), di hofnung un der tsukunft, nor ich hob keyn dreyst nit fortusleygen meine gute eltern aza zach—far a froyentsimer iz es a tsu shvere oyfgabe. Git mir a rat (an eytse) vi dos zol geshen, ich ken dos nit, dos kost mir mein gezunt un eich—eier geduld.

Eier Ana Sheynfinkl

41. PHILLIP TO ANNA

Bialistok, 14 April 1903

It was with the greatest impatience that I awaited your letter and with the greatest pleasure that I read it. The magnet—as it is described—has the property that whatever it touches, so long as it is metal, acquires magnetic force. But "love" is stronger by far: it sanctifies and refines everything, everything. . . . The paper of your letter and the envelope have a value to me that knows no equal. Your two letters are now like my own.

The advice you ask for I can give only if you will concur with it. Either I myself will ask your good parents for your hand as soon as you give me your consent to it in writing, or else I will send a matchmaker in my parents' name. They know a little about our relationship and are extremely happy that my choice has fallen upon you, dear Anna.

Write me which plan you like best, and I will execute it forthwith.

Your Phillip Eichhorn

Mit dem grestn ungeduld hob ich eier briv ervart un mit dem gresten fargenigen gelezen. Der magnes—vi es iz bashriben—hot di eygenshaft az tsu vos er rirt zich tsu oyb dos iz nur metal bakumt es magnes-kraft, di "libe" iz ober fil shtarker: zi farheylikt un farteiert ales ales. . . . Dos papir fun eier briv un der konvert hoben bei mir aza vert vos es git gor keyn gleichen dertsu. Eiere tsvey briv zeinen bei mir yetst mein eygens.

Dem rat vos ir bet ken ich eich geben, nor oyb ir vet tsu im einshtimen. Ich vel oder zelbst bei eiere gute eltern eier hand beten gleich vi ir vet mir eier einshtimung dertsu shreiben; oder ich vel a shadchen in nomen fun meine eltern shiken. Zey visen a bisl fun undzere farheltenishen un zeinen hechst tsufriden vos mein val iz af eich, libe Ana, gefalen.

Shreibt mir velcher plan gefelt eich beser, dem vel ich ungezamt ton.

Eier Filip Eichhorn

42. ANNA TO PHILLIP

Grodno, 16 April 1903

Dear, precious Phillip,

Chance selected your first plan, and so I nominate it, too. Your letter arrived just when I was out of the house. My good mother took it from the mailman and—not intending anything—she opened it and read it. Naturally, she conveyed it all to my father. And when I returned home, my father called me in to his study and there he, as well as my mother, explained to me that they know your family in the best sense, that my father also knows you well, and they both told me quite openly that they consent to our wish.

So, dear Phillip, come and talk to my good parents yourself—our happiness rests in our own hands. . . .

Your Anna Scheinfinkel

PS: Sincerest congratulations!

Liber teierster Filip!

Der tsufal hot eier ershtn plan oysgekliben alzo bashtim ich es oych. Eier briv iz ongekumen grade ven ich bin tsu hoyze nit geven. Mein gute muter hot es fun briventreger opgenumen, di—nit meynendik keyn zach—hot im geefent un gelezen. Zelbstfarshtendik az zi hot ales mein foter ibergegeben. Un az ich bin tsu hoyze gekumen hot mir der foter in zein kabinet areingerufen un dorten hot er, oych di muter mir erklert dos zey kenen eier familye fun bester zeite, dos der foter ken eich oych gut, un zey beyde hoben mir ofen gezogt dos zey shtimen ein tsu undzer vunsh.

Alzo, liber Filip, kumt un ret mit meine gute eltern zelbst— undzer glik iz bei undz in di hend. . . .

Eier Ana Sheynfinkl

P.S. Ich gratulir eich fun tifen hartsen!

Letters between Fiancés

43. TO ONE'S FIANCÉE

Subalk, 15 May 1903

My betrothed and love of my heart,

This letter is the first since our joyous betrothal; in it, my dearest, you will find nothing new. You will only find the words which you have already heard from me many times and which I hope you will forever hear from me, namely, that you are my joy, my desire and my life; that my love for you is unbounded.

You are a good few hours distant from me by train; but, like the sun which is far away from the earth yet gives it light, so give me light although you are far away. You are here with me, with me in my head, with me in my heart—you are mine.

Your loving fiancé, who waits for you to write with the greatest impatience,

Shimon Goldberg

Hartsensgelibte broyte!

Der briv iz der ershter noch undzer gliklechen farlobung. In ir, mein teierste, vestu keyne neies gefinen. Du vest nor gefinen in im di verter, velche du host fun mir shoyn fil mol gehert un velkhe ich hof du vest eybik fun mir heren, dos heyst dos du bist mein glik, mein vunsh un mein leben; dos mein libe tsu dir iz on a grenets.

Du bist zogar veit fun mir eynike shtunden tseit mit dem ban tsu reizen; ober vi di zun velche iz zeyer veit fun di erd un baleicht ir doch, zo baleicht's du mir obvoyl du bist fun veiten. Du bist bei mir, bei mir in kop, bei mir in hartsen—du bist meine.

Dein libender broytigam, velcher ervartet dein shreiben mit dem gresten ungeduld,

Shimen Goldberg

44. REPLY

Lomza, 21 May 1903

My dear Shimon,

Your dear letter stirred me with delight. There is nothing I can write in reply. Can I write anything other than what you wrote to me? It would be quite right of me if I were to copy out your letters, sign them, and dispatch them to you—only if in that way we might always send the same letter to one another. And so I must write you something else, but the purpose is the same: I love you deeply in my heart, you are the only thing of interest to me, you are mine.

Write as often as you can, as reading your letters is now your future bride's full-time occupation.

Naomi Wechsler

Mein lieber Shimen!

Dein liber briv hot mir baroysht mit glik. Keyn antvort hob ich dir nit tsu shreiben. Ken ich dir den vos andersh shreiben vi du tsu mir? Ich volt richtik geton ven ich volt deine briv kopiren, untershreiben zey, un dir opshiken; nor oyb azoy volten mir imer nor dem eyn briv eyner dem anderen shiken. Alzo muz ich dir etvos andersh shreiben, ober der tsil iz der zelbiker: ich lib dir tif fun hartsen, du bist dos eyntsike vos interesirt mir, du bist meiner.

Shreib vos mer, den lezen deine briv iz yetst dos gantse basheftikung fun dein broyte.

Nomi Veksler

45. SHIMON TO NAOMI

Subalk, 25 May 1903

Sweet, delightful Naomi!

Your words are pearls and diamonds. Your prose sounds like the best of music to my ears. Oh, how false, how baseless is the view of philosophers who say that everything on earth is nothingness! No, the world is a paradise for those who have the fortune to love and be loved.

I only know that ever since I have known you, my whole world has been a garden of delights, everything I look at rejoices, everything is like me—blissful!

There is but one small cloud in my heaven—that we are going far from one another, that to have you next to me I must make use of fantasy. . . . But that will not last long. In three months' time, you will be mine and by my side. . . . How I am already living that blissful time!

Yours forever,

Shimon

Zise eingeneme Nomi!

Perl un brilyantn zeinen deine verter un vi di beste muzik klingen deine prozen. Ah, vi falsh, vi ungrindlik iz der meynung fun di filozofen vos zogen az ales af der velt iz gor nisht! Neyn, di velt iz a gan-eyden far di vos hoben dem glik tsu liben un gelibt tsu zein.

Ich veys nor az zeit ich hob dir derkent iz mir di gantse velt a lust-gortn, ales af vos ich kuk freit zich, ales iz vi ich— gliklech!

Es iz nur eyn kleyner volken af mein himel—vos mir zeinen veit eyner fun tsveytn, vos um tsu hoben dir leben zich muz ich di fantazye onvenden. . . . Ober dos vet lang nit gedoyren. Noch drei monatn un du bizt meine un neben mir. . . . Vi derleb ich shoyn di glikleche tseit.

Deiner af eybik,

Shimen

46. NAOMI TO SHIMON

Lomza, 15 June 1903

My dear fiancé,

You are, my dearest, an artist! You do not write with a pen but with a heart, with a heart filled with a love hot as fire. The day I receive your letter I lock myself in my room so that none may mar my bliss. I read your letters ten times over and discover in them more and still more . . . In my sleep I read them. I read them by day, and when do I not read them? Ah, I exclaim from the depths of my heart, how I am already living the golden time when I will no longer call you, as now, "fiancé," but something else, something hotter. . . .

Entirely yours,

Naomi

Mein liber broytigam!

Du bizt, mein teierster, a kinstler! Du shreibst nit mit a feder nor mit harts, mit harts ful mit libe heyse vi feier. Dem tog vos ich bakum dein briv farshlis ich zech in mein tsimer, keyner zol mir mein glik nit shtern. Ich lez deine briv tsendliker mol un gefin in zey ales mer un mer . . . Fun shlof lez ich zey. Bei tog lez ich zey un ven lez ich zey nit? Ah! Shrei ich oys fun tifen hartsen— vi derleb ich shoyn di goldene tseit az ich vel dir shoyn mer nit rufen vi yetst "broytigam" nor andersh un heyser. . . .

In gantsen deine,

Nomi

47. TO ONE'S FIANCÉE

Petrokov, 3 August 1903

My dear Lisa,

The thought that we now belong to one another, that I can hope and have the right to say that you are mine—makes me happy. I have never known such joy, I have never felt so good as I do now, since we have been engaged. I feel that I am quite another person!
I feel now that everything ever written about love is true and sacred. This is the best medicine to make life sweet and give it worth; without love there is no life. Without love there is no pleasure!
I have no words for happiness, there is nothing further I can write about it. Just in order that my first letter should not be too brief, I am adding these words: If this world has people who understand their happiness, first among them is

Your Joseph Oppenheim

Meine teiere Liza!

Der gedank dos mir geheren yetst eyner dem tsveytn, dos ich ken hofen un hob recht tsu zogen dos du bist meine—macht mir gliklech. Ich bin keyn mol azoy freylech nit geven, ich hob zich keyn mol azoy gut nit gefilt vi yetst tseit mir zeinen farlobt, ich fil dos ich bin gor an ander mentsh!
Ich fil yetst az ales vos men hot vegen libe geshriben iz emes

un heylik. Dis iz der bester medikament (heilmitel) dem leben tsu farzisen un im a vert tsutsugeben, on libe iz keyn leben. On libe iz keyn fargenigen!

Fun glik hob ich keyn verter nit, fun glik ken ich mer nit shreiben. Nor mein ershter briv zol nit tsu kurts zein, derleyg ich noch di verter: Ven es iz do af der velt mentshen vos farshteyn zeyer glik, iz der ershter fun zey

Dein Yozef Openheim

48. REPLY

Slonim, 10 August 1903

My Joseph, my only,

The greatest wish I have entertained in my life has been attained; you, my betrothed, understand how to love and are worthy of love. But "when one attains one wish, another one comes right along." My second wish is now that we should always have these feelings for each other and that we should stay with these thoughts. . . .

Write to me as often as you can; pleasure is a thing that everyone desires in large amounts, and "now" only your letters can give me pleasure.

Forever yours,

Lisa Zborski

Meiner, nor meiner Yozef!

Mein gresten vunsh vos ich hob in mein leben gehat, hob ich ereicht, du mein broytigam farshteyst vi tsu liben un bist libensvertik. Nor "ven men ereicht eyn vunsh, kumt gleich a tsveyter." Mein tsveyter vunsh iz yetst az mir zolen ale mol di gefilen hoben eyner tsum tsveytn un mir zolen bei yetstike gedanken bleiben. . . .

Shreib mir vos mer; fargenigen vinsht zich yeder fil tsu hoben, un fargenigen farshafen mir "yetst" nor deine briv.

Af eybik deine,

Liza Zborski

49. TO ONE'S FIANCÉ

Dvinsk, 8 September 1903

Dear fiancé Shelomo,

This is my last letter to you. For the last time I am calling you fiancé—in two days I will already be calling you by another name. . . . In reply to this letter of mine, I am waiting with open arms for you yourself, you with your dear parents, your sisters and brothers and good friends. Tuesday will be the best day of my life, the day when I make the step that a person makes and wants to make only once in a lifetime, for the whole of that lifetime. May God grant that it lead us both to happiness!
Adieu, my dearest, until Tuesday!

Your betrothed, who is thinking of you only,

Helena Mintz

Liber, teierster broytigam Shloyme!

Dos iz mein letster briv tsu dir. Dem letstn mol ruf ich dir broytigam—noch tsvey teg vel ich dir shoyn mit an ander nomen rufen. . . . als antvort af mein briv dizen, ervart ich mit ofene orems dir zelbst, dir mit deine libe eltern, deine shvester un brider un gute freind. Dinstik vet zein der bester tog fun mein leben, der tog in velchen ich mach dem shrit vos a mentsh

macht un vil machn nor eyn mol in leben af a gantsen leben. Gib Got es zol undz beyden tsum glik firen!
   Adie, mein teierster biz dinstik!

Dein broyte, velche tracht nor vegen dir,

Helena Mints

50. FROM AN EX-FIANCÉE

Tukum, 1 July 1903

Dear friend,

You have been the only one to know of my relationship with Leon Gampyofitz, only you knew when our passionate love began three years ago before he set off for his studies, and you are the only one to whom I now pour out my heart, when love has flown. . . . Yes, my friend, I am safely over it, thank God. . . . It has taken a heavy toll of my health, but it was worth it—I am forever fortunate that I realized in time, that is to say, when I could have agreed to the whole matter with one word. I had eyes of glass. I noticed nothing or else looked on the good side of things. I was deluded, deceived, and enticed—but enough! I convinced myself in time how depraved he is, how false and base, and was saved—I am free. I am now going to think things over with a calm head and take a rest from three years of worry. Ah, three years, three years of my life and wellbeing!

Your friend,

Sonia Eilbogarten

Beste freindin!

Du bist di eyntsike geven vos host gevust fun ale meine farheltnise mit Leon Gampyofitz, du nor host gevust ven undzer heyse libe hot zich ongefangen mit drei yor tsurik eyder er iz shtudiren geforen, un du bist di eyntsike, far velche ich gis yetst oys mein harts, als di libe iz oys. . . . Yo, meine freindin, ich bin Got tsu danken ariber gekumen. . . . Es hot mir fil gezunt gekost, es iz ober vert—ich bin imer gliklech vos ich hob zich doch arumgezen batseiten, dos heyst ven mit eyn vort hob ich es oych gekent opmachen. Ich hob gehat glezerne oygen. Ich hob keyn zach nit bamerkt oder fun der guter zeite gerechent. Ich bin geven farblent, farfirt un farnart—ober genug! Ich hob doch batseiten ibertseigt zich vi veit fardorben er iz, vi veit falsh un nidertrechtik, un bin geretet—ich bin frei. Ich vel zich yetst mit a ruike kop batrachten un oysruen far di fardreyenish, velche hot drei yor gedoyert. Ah, drei yor; drei yor gezunt un leben!

Dein freindin,

Sonye Eylboygarten

51. REPLY

Kalvariya, 5 July 1903

Dear Sonia,

Your letter came as no surprise—I always expected such an end to it. I happened to run into the brat in a few places, as well as at two weddings. What shall I tell you? Such depravity is a rare thing! We always used to be astonished at you for not seeing it, for not noticing. You only have the Good Lord to thank for opening your eyes in time. It serves him right with his studies, with his lies—life is worth more. . . .

Your friend,

Fanye Mushkat

Teierste Sonye!

Dein briv hot mir nit iberasht—ich hob aza ende ale mol ervart. Ich hob grod in eynike shtelen getrofen zich mit dem tachshit, oych oyf tsvey chasenes. Vos zol ich dir zogen? Azoy fardorben iz a zeltenheyt! Mir flegen zich shtendik nit kenen farvunderen oyf dir vos du zest nit, vos du bamerkst nit. Nor du megst Gut Got danken vos er hot dir batseiten deine oygen geefent. A kapore er mit zein shtudiren, mit zein falshkeyt— der leben iz teierer. . . .

Dein freindin,

Fanye Mushkat

Letters between Husband and Wife

52. A HUSBAND TO A WIFE

New York, 3 November 1903

Dear, sweet Chanale,

You have been waiting impatiently for my first letter after going away. I can sense that very well. You would already have wished to know how I am and if I have attained my objective. So I am writing to you that I have been successful—I have arrived in New York at a good time: I immediately got a good position in a big textiles business. My wages are, for the time being, still uncertain; they first have to be persuaded how capable I am; but the two of us know, don't we, how well I worked in Moscow and how my boss respected me. People appear to be good-natured, and I hope that they will be pleased with me and I with them. And that is all my wish.

Your loving husband,

Ber Lieberman

Libe gute Chane'le!

Do host mit ungeduld gevart af mein ershten briv noch mein opreizen. Ich fil dos zeyer gut. Du volst shoyn gevolt visen vos mit mir iz un tsi hob ich mein tsil ereicht. Alzo shreib ich dir az mir hot zich eingegeben—ich bin tsu der guter tseit noch Nyu-York ongekumen: ich hob gleich a feine shtele bakumen in a groysen manufaktur gesheft. Mein loyn iz noch derveile unbashtimt, zey darfen zich frier ibertseigen vi veit feyik ich bin; nor mir beyde visen doch vi gut ich hob gearbet in Moskve un vi geacht ich bin geven bei mein printsipal. Di mentshen sheinen tsu zein gute, un ich farhof az zey velen fun mir tsufriden zein un oych ich fun zey. Un dos iz mein vunsh.

Dein dich libender man,

Ber Liberman

53. REPLY

Babroisk, 7 November 1903

My dearest husband,

Your thoughts did not deceive you. The pious do not await the Messiah with such impatience as I awaited your letter. And no wonder. We were, to be sure, living quite nicely in Moscow, we had food in plenty and were in debt to no one. But a calamity came upon us and in the space of twenty-four hours our quiet life was disrupted and totally shattered. . . . We ran (or, rather, we were driven) as if by a fire wherever we could see to go. In the unhappy few months living in Babroisk, we ate the skin off our bones, we pawned and we mortgaged everything we had, until you had the idea of going to New York to find a job of some kind. So, ought I not to have awaited your letter like the accused awaits his trial?

Now I praise God, my only wish is that you should make a nice impression on the boss of the business, and then, please God, we will be able to begin forgetting about our troubles and maybe one day recount them in good times.

Your adoring wife,

Hanna Lieberman

Teierster man meiner!

Deine gedanken hoben dir nit opgenart: Di frume vartn nit af meshiech'n mit aza ungeduld vi ich hob af dein briv gevart. Un es iz keyn vunder nit. Mir hoben doch in Moskve gelebt gut un sheyn, gehat lebensmitel bekoved un keynem nit shuldik geven. Es iz ober a tsore gekumen un hot undzer ruiken leben in farloyf fun fir un tsvantsik sho tsushtert un tseruinirt in gantsen. . . . Mir zeinen gelofen (oder beser: men hot undz geyogt) vi fun feier vu di oygen hoben getrogen. Mir hoben in di unglikleche por monaten voynendik in Babroisk oyfgegesen di hoyt fun di beyner, ales farzetst, un farmashkent, biz dir iz eingefalen noch Nyu-York tsu foren avelche shtele tsu gefinen. Nu, hob ich nit gedarft varten af dein briv vi a farshuldikter af zein mishpet?

Yetst loyb ich Got, ich vinsh zich nor du zolst cheyn gefinen in di oygen fun dein shef (balebos fun gesheft) un dan velen mir im yirtse hashem on undzere tsores kenen onheyben fargesen un amol noch fileicht in freyden dertseylen.

Deine dich shetsende froy,

Chane Liberman

54. A WIFE TO A HUSBAND

Kishinev, 8 July 1903

My dear husband Yitzchok,

Today is three months to the day since our calamity. Today I paid my third visit to our son's grave, and an amazing thing—he gave me the same answer from over there, from the Hereafter, as we are given down here.
One no longer cries out at the pains. Not because they have now completely healed. Absolutely not! But fine membranes have been, one might say, stretched out by a hand from above, the cuts have been sewn up. Yet down below there is still matter, and up above a twisted face. . . . One forgets the dead. But here we still have the living left without life. And living woes live and grow. . . .
What is with you there? Why do you write so little and so infrequently? Have you already achieved something there? Write me about everything.

Your faithful wife,

Libo Nevelsohn

Mein teierer man Yitschok!

Heint iz punkt drei chadoshim noch undzer churben. Heint bin ich dem driten mol oyf undzer zuns keyver geven, un merkverdik—er hot mir fun dorten, fun oylem hoemes, dem zelbiken entfer gegeben vos men git undz do.

Men shreit shoyn nit mer oyf di veytiken. Nit veil zey zeinen shoyn in gantsen oysgeheylt. Neyn un neyn! Nor es zeinen etvos fun oyben fartseygen gevoren dine heitlech, es zeinen farneyt gevoren di shniten. Unten iz noch ober do materye un oyben a farheykerte ponim. . . . Der toyter vert fargesen. Ober bei undz iz noch do toyte gebliben lebedike. Un lebedike tsores— leben un vaksen. . . .

Vos iz dorten mit dir? Far vos shreibstu azoy veynik un nit oft? Hostu zich dorten shoyn tsu vos dershlogen? Shreib mir fun als.

Dein treie froy,

Libo Nevelson

55. REPLY

New York, 23 July 1903

My dear wife Libo,

To set your mind at rest, I am writing to tell you that here, thank God, I am earning some money. So far I have not sent you any money, but not, Heaven forbid, because I do not have any, but because, firstly, I left you with one hundred rubles, did I not, and, secondly, I do not want to send American dollars to you. One needs to go to get American money, rather than receive it in the mail and spend it. I am getting settled here and in the next letter I will be sending you a ticket for the boat—come over to me here and breathe some fresh air like everyone else; see how they live and live a life also. Here a Jew can also live, here everyone is safe and everyone is equal. . . .

The reason I am not writing much is that in America not only money is expensive but time and words, too. Here you say what you mean, so one ought not to say much or write much.

Your husband who awaits your arrival with happiness,

Yitzchok Nevelsohn

Meine teiere froy Libo!

Tsu dein baruikung shreib ich dir dos ich fardin do, danken Got. Ich hob dir keyn gelt noch biz yetst nit geshikt, nit chas vesholem veil ich hob nit, nor veil ershtens hob ich dir hundert rubel ibergelozen, un tsveytens vil ich dir ahin keyn amerikaner tolers nit shiken. Noch amerikaner gelt darf men foren un nit bakumen zey durch post un oysgeben. Ich order zich do ein un vel dir in tsveyten briv a shifs karte shiken—kum tsu mir un otem do, vi ale, freie luft; ze vi men lebt un leb oych. Do ken a yid oych leben, do zeinen ale zicher, ale gleich. . . .

Dos vos ich shreib veynik iz nor veil in Amerika iz nit nor gelt teier, nor oych tseit un verter. Do ret men vos men meynt, alzo darfen veynik reden oych shreiben.

Dein man vos vart oyf dein kumen mit glik,

Yitschok Nevelson

56. A HUSBAND TO A WIFE

Boston, 5 May 1903

My dearest beloved wife!

Yes, I'm into my second year here now. I must have written you and received from you a dozen letters already, yet each time I write to you I feel a particular delight. It is as if I were speaking to you aloud. Sometimes a sigh escapes from deep down in my heart—I recall the happy time when we were together, how well we used to spend those times I was free from work—but what can a person do? One has to be satisfied with the way things are. I hope the situation will not drag out for long. With God's help I will bring you across to me when this summer is over, and we will be together once more and lead a quiet and peaceful life. Take heart, look after yourself: The time will fly—the bad will pass, and with the new year good times will come upon us together.

Your husband, who thinks of you alone,

Dovid Pinskoy

Libste teierste froy meine!

Ich bin doch shoyn do di andere yor, ich hob doch dir shoyn tsendliker briv geshriben oych erhalten fun dir, un doch fil ich yeder mol ven ich shreib dir, a bazunderen fargenigen: Mir ducht zech az ich red mit dir mindlik. Tseitenveiz ganvet zech aroys a sifts tif, tif fun hartsen—ich dermon zech di glikleche tseit ven mir zenen tsuzamen gevezen, vi gut mir flegen zech farbrengen di tseit, in velche ich bin frei fun arbet gevezen . . . vos ken a mentsh ober machen? Men muz tsufriden zein vi es iz. Ich hof az es vet zech lang der tsushtand nit tsihen, ich vel dir mit gots hilf noch ende heintiken zumer opnemen tsu zech, un mir velen veiter tsuzamen zein un firen a shtilen ruhiken leben. Fas mut, ze zech tsu: di tseit vet ariber fliyen—di shlecht's vet avekgeyn un mit dem neiem yor tsuzamen vet af uns gut's kumen.

Dein man, vos tracht nor vegen dir,

Dovid Pinskoy

57. REPLY

Kovno, 20 May 1903

My good husband!

Your letter of May 5, which I received today, is the twenty-eighth; I have now received twenty-eight letters from you and read them several times over; but I read it like I read the first letter, meaning to say that I cried as I read it. I miss you with every step I take, and I can no longer understand how I was so foolish as to allow you to go away to America. What is my life without you? Believe me that it is not worth a cent! Today you can picture how great was my joy when I read in your letter that we'll see an end in a few months' time to our present chaotic life! My tears here have already turned to tears of joy. Please God, your words should soon be fulfilled and we should yet have joy in place of suffering.

Your devoted wife,

Sore Pinskoy

Guter man meiner,

Dein briv fun finften mei, velchen ich hob heint erhalten, iz der acht-un-tsvantsikter; acht-un-tsvantsik briv hob ich fun dir shoyn erhalten un tsu eynike mol gelezen; doch hob ich im vi dem ershten briv gelezen, dos heyst gelezen un geveynt. Du felst mir af yeder trit, un ich farshtey yetst nit vi bin ich narish geven un hob dan eingeshtimt du zolst in Amerike avek foren. Vos iz mein leben on dir? Gloyb mir az es iz keyn shiling nit vert! Heint kenstu zech farshtelen vi veit mein freyd iz geven az ich hob in dein briv gelezen az es vet in a por monaten arum nemen an ende fun dem itstiken tsevarfenem leben! Do zeinen shoyn meine treren geven freyde-treren. Gib got deine verter zolen mekuyem veren un mir zolen noch hoben freyd far undzer leid.

Dein dir ibergegebene froy,

Sore Pinskoy

58. A WIFE TO A HUSBAND

Ponevezh, 7 April 1903

Dearest Shelomo,

Your letters are my cure for everything. When I receive a letter from you about your health, I am already content. But you, my dear, are a miserly apothecary—you dole out the letters to me infrequently and you write very sparingly. Is it right to do a thing like this? Tell me yourself, must it be like this?

I myself and our beautiful children, may they be spared, are well, thank God. They all ask to send you their sincerest regards and long for you no less than I.

A few days ago we had regards from you via someone passing through, someone called Levine. He knows you well and says you also know him well—you are lodging in the same courtyard.

To end my letter, I have to write you an important piece of news. In a few weeks I'm expecting a very nice guest. . . . I figure that on account of him you will soon be seeing your wife,

Chaya Perlman

Teierster Shloyme!

Deine briv zeinen bei mir a heilmitel fun ales, az ich derhalt fun dir a briv fun dein gezunt, bin ich shoyn tsufriden. Nor du, mein liber, bist a karger apteyker—du teylst mir tsu di briv zelten un shreibst zeyer veynik. Iz dos recht azoy? Zog aleyn, darf azoy zein?

Ich, oych undzere gerotene kinderlech, zolen leben, zeinen danken got gezunt, zey lozen dir ale grisen zeyer hartslech un benken noch dir nit veyniker far mir.

Mit eynike teg tsurik hoben mir fun dir a grus gehat durch a durchforer, eyner a Levin; er ken dir gut un zogt az du kenst im oych gut—ir kvartirt af eyn hoyf.

Tsum ende mein briv muz ich dir a vichtike neies shreiben: ich ervart in a por vochen arum zeyer a guten gast. . . . Ich rechen az tsulib im vet zich mit dir in gichen zen dein froy,

Chaye Perlman

59. REPLY

Kursenai, 12 April 1903

My dear, beloved wife,

I am not to blame, Heaven forbid, for my letters being so infrequent and so brief. Now is the height of the seasonal trade, and there are days when I don't eat a thing till the evening, and on evenings that I'm exhausted I quite often fall asleep with my clothes on—that's how busy I am. So, imagine for yourself whether I can write frequently and fully.

Give regards to our two dear little children. I am awaiting the dear visitor with the greatest impatience; please God, he should be a delightful new arrival. Then we will most definitely see one another. Have everything ready for the visitor!

Your ever adoring husband,

Shelomo Perlman

Libe teierste froy!

Ich bin oser nit shuldik in dem vos meine briv zeinen azoy zelten un kurts, es iz itster di rechte tseit fun sezon gesheft, un es treft teg vos ich es gor nit biz ovnt, un ovnt az ich bin farmatert fal ich shlofen gants oft nit oysgeton—azoy bin ich basheftikt. Nu, farshtey aleyn ken ich oft un fil shreiben.

Gris undzere tsvey libe kinderlech. Af dem liben gast vart ich mit dem gresten ungeduld: Gib Got er zol mit fargenigen kumen, dan velen mir zich zen gants bashtimt. Hob ales ongegreyt far dem gast!

Dein dich eybik libender man,

Shloyme Perlman

60. A HUSBAND TO A WIFE

Kremenchug, 15 November 1903

My dearest wife,

I was delighted to read your letter, in which you write to me that you, as well as our dear little children, are missing me and do not stop mentioning me. Believe me, my dear, I am also thinking only of you all and feel lonesome here without you.
 I will be coming home soon for two weeks. Then I will enjoy you.

Also loving you ardently,

Zalman Gitelson

Teierste froy meine!

Mit freyd hob ich dein briv gelezen, in velchen du shreibst mir az du oych undzere libe kinderlech benken vegen mir un heren nit oyf mir tsu dermonen. Gloyb mir, mein teierste, az ich tracht oych nor vegen eich un fil zich elent do on eich.
 Ich vel in gichen aheym kumen oyf tsvey vochen, dan vet zich mit eich freyen eier oych heys libender.

Zalmen Gitelson

61. IN ANOTHER MANNER

My dear, sweet wife,

I cannot fully express the pleasure I have from your letters. I will convey my feelings to you orally. The wishes from our dear child are the only thing in the world that can rival your writing—you and the child, the child and you, this is all that lights up my life and gives it a charm.

Be well, my dears, another two months and I will be coming to you for the holiday. Then it will be a real holiday for us all.

Your husband,

Michael Schneersohn

Gute libe froy meine!

Dem fargenigen vos ich hob fun deine briv ken ich dir nit oysshreiben. Ich vel dir meine gefile mindlech ibergeben. Der grus fun undzer liben kind iz dos eyntsikes in der velt vos konkurirt mit dein shreiben—du un dos kind, dos kind un du, ot dos iz ales vos erleicht mein leben un macht im reitsendik.

Zeit gezunt, meine libe, noch tsvey monaten vel ich tsu eich kumen oyf yontef, dan vet bei undz alemen zein an emeser yontef.

Dein man,

Michoel Shnerson

62. A WIFE TO HER HUSBAND

Dubbelin, 10 July 1903

My dear spouse Isaac,

This is the fourth week that I have been here. I eat and drink and take walks by the shore—everything might have been all right, except that I am short of many things. You should see how respectable ladies turn out here! It is a delight to watch. And so, I am short of three items and then I will have everything—four nice, good dresses, a rain coat, a few bathing costumes, an iron, a white silk parasol and the like. You understand, of course, that I need money besides, as everything here is costly, only money is cheap. . . .

I am sure you will only be able to come out here in a few weeks, so dispatch me money for everything as soon as you possibly can.

Your wife,

Rosa Shochadkewitz

Bester gemal Izak!

Es iz di firte voch zind ich bin do, ich es un trink un shpatsir am shtrand—es volt ales gut geven, nor mir felt fil zachen. Du volst zen vi onshtendike damen geyn do aroys! Es iz a fargenigen tsu zen. Alzo um ales tsu hoben, felt mir drei—fir sheyne gute kleyder, a regen mantel, a por bode-kostyumen, a pres, a veiser zeidener zonenshirm un dos gleichen. Farshteyst doch az ich darf oyf dem hoben gelt, vorem als iz do teier, nor gelt iz bilik. . . .

Du vest gevis kenen kumen aher ersht in eynike vochen arum, alzo shik mir vos gicher aroys gelt oyf ales.

Dein froy,

Roze Shochadkevits

63. REPLY

Dvinsk, 22 July 1903

Dearest Rosa,

I have been in no hurry to answer your letter thus far, and now I am only sending you a letter. Do you know why? Because I am convinced that you are not asking for anything that is essential. One can get by without them and be perfectly well. One does not make the trip to Dubbelin for the high style and the display, one goes to recover, to relax.

"Respectable ladies," you write, turn out there beautifully dressed; but I think they should be called by a quite different word: spendthrifts, quirkies, or bankrupts. A true "respectable woman" only spends money on what she "needs," on things she cannot do without, but not on trifles, because that's how "she" goes and that's how "others" go—that is not what I call "respectable"! . . .

We are no millionaires, no empty aristocrats who buy their aristocracy from milliners and in the off-the-peg stores. We are ordinary people; I do not "wish" to go bust, nor "will" I, with God's help. One has to do what one has to do, and what is unnecessary is needless!

Unshakable in my opinions,

Your husband Isaac

Teierste Roze!

Ich hob zich nit geeilt dir oyf dein briv tsu antvorten biz yetst, oich yetst shik ich dir nor a briv aleyn, veystu far vos? Veil ich bin ibertseigt az du betst nit keyn neytike zachen: Men ken oyskumen on zey un zein gezunt. In Dubbelin fort men nit noch dem shtat un puts, men fort um zich tsu erholen, zich oystsuruen.

"Onshtendike froyen"—shreibstu, geyn dorten aroys zeyer sheyn gekleydet; ich meyn ober az men darf zey gants andersh rufen: oysbrengerkes, modnitses, oder onzetserkes. An emese "onshtendike froy" farbroycht gelt nor oyf vos men "muz," on vos men ken zich nit bageyn; ober nit oyf dudes, veil azoy geyt "di" un azoy "yene"—geyn, nit dos heyst bei mir "onshtendik"! . . .

Mir zeinen nit keyn milyoneren, nit keyn puste aristokraten, velche koyfen zeyer aristokratizm bei di putsenmacherinen un in di gesheften fun fartike kleyder. Mir zenen geveynleche mentshen. Onzetsen "vil" ich nit, un "vel" nit mit Gots hilf; vos men darf darf men, un vos es iz nit neytik—darf men nit!

Dein man vos bleibt bei zein meynung,

Izak

64. ROSA TO ISAAC

My dear Isaac,

Don't be so stingy to me. All in all, how on earth can a person have it all so worked out what they must have and what is excess? You ought not to count what I am asking for as excessive. I know our standing perfectly well. Your proof is that a few years back I never used to think about a spa or about grooming. Now that God has helped us for a few years and we can do it, why should I be any worse than anyone else? Am I a common woman off the street, then?

So grant me my request, suppose that you possess a few hundred rubles less, don't make me any hassle, and see to it that I should be able to get hold of everything.

Your wife,

Rosa Shochadkewitz

Teierster Izak *meiner!*

Zei nit azoy karg far mir; iber hoypt vi iz dos a mentsh azoy oysgerechent vos men muz un vos iz iberik? Dos vos ich bet darfstu nit rechnen far iberik. Ich veys gants gut undzer shtand. A baveiz hostu az mit eynike yor tsurik fleg ich gor nit trachten vegen a bod un vegen tualet. Yetst az Got hot undz tseit eynike yor geholfen, az mir kenen dos oysfiren, far vos zol ich nit zein tsu leiten gleich? Bin ich den a yente fun gas?

Alzo erfil mein farlang, zol dir duchten az du farmogst mit eynike hundert rubel veyniker, mach mir nit on keyn fardros un ze ich zol ales kenen shafen.

Dein froy,

Roze Shochadkevits

65. A HUSBAND TO HIS WIFE

My dear, beloved wife,

You are no doubt worried that you have not had a letter from me for some weeks. Believe me when I say that it has caused me no end of upset; but what should I do when I still have nothing to write? It is good to write cheerful news and cheerful letters, but if for the time being I can only give you hope, if I have no good news—what should I write to you?

Times are very bad, business is quiet, and no one wants to take on new people or has any need for them. It has been suggested that I become a *melamed*[33] in a village, where, in exchange for teaching three children, I would receive board, lodging, and twenty rubles a month. But I have no interest in becoming a tutor; to me it seems like the worst of all possible things. What do you advise? If you agree, I will accept it forthwith. What can one do? "A drowning man grabs at a knife."

Your husband,

Pinchas Gilbo

Teiere libe froy meine!

Du bist gevis umruik vos du host shoyn tseit eynike vochen fun mir keyn briv gehat. Gloyb mir dos ich hob derfun nit veynik

---

33. Tutor, especially in religious subjects.

fardros, nor vos zol ich ton az ich hob fort nit vos tsu shreiben? Es iz gut tsu shreiben freyleche neies, freyleche briv, ober ven ich ken nor hofnung geben dir forloyfik, ven keyn gute neies hob ich nit—vos zol ich dir shreiben?

Di tseit iz zeyer shlecht, di gesheften zeinen shtil, un neie mentshen vil keyner nit onnemen un er darf zey nit. Men leygt mir for a melamed veren oyf a yishuv, vu far mein lernen mit drei kinder vel ich tish, kvatir un tsvantsik rubel monatlech bakumen. Nor mir vilt zich keyn melamed nit zein, mir ducht zich az dos iz shoyn di ergste zach. Vi iz dein eytse? Oyb du shtimst tsu, nem ich dos gleich on, vos ken men machen? "Der vos trenkt zech, chapt zich far a meser."

Dein man,

Pinches Gilbo

66. REPLY

My dearest husband,

In reply to your query, I advise you to accept the post of *melamed* immediately. After all, you know both languages: Hebrew and Russian. You will certainly know how to teach children. Don't they say that "a *melamed* can also be dumb"? You can talk, thank God, you will no doubt make the childish parents happy, and then you, too, will be happy.

I must tell you that the name "*melamed*" no longer has a stigma attached to it. There are already *melameds* in short coats, in boots with galoshes, and others are even starting to wear top hats on the Sabbath. . . . It can indeed be that they know even less than the *melameds* with long sidelocks and rank beneath them in many matters. But it has already become the fashion today that you should not call yourself *melamed* but *lerer*,[34] call yourself whatever suits you, just earn some money for yourself and your family. With time, God can also send us along some better business.

Your faithful wife,

Perl Gilbo

---

34. Teacher.

Teierer man meiner!

Als antvort oyf dein onfrage, rate ich dir di shtele fun melamdus gleich ontsunemen. Du kenst doch gut beyde shprachen: hebreish un rusish. Du vest gevis farshteyn vi mit kinder tsu lernen. Men zogt doch az "a melamed ken zein a shtumer oych," du kenst danken Got reden, du vest gevis tsufriden shtelen di kindershe elteren un dan vestu oych tsufriden zein.

Ich muz dir zogen az itster iz shoyn arop di cherpe fun dem nomen "melamed," es iz shoyn do melamdim in kurtse rek, in shtivel mit kalasen, un andere chapen zogar onton shabes a tsilinderhut. . . . Es ken take zein az zey kenen noch veyniker far di lange peyesdike melamdim un shteyn in fil zachen nidriker far zey; ober azoy iz shoyn heint in mode arein, ruf zich nit "melamed" nor "lerer," ruf zich vi dir past, nor fardin far zich un far dein familye. Mit der tseit ken Got geben besere gesheften oych.

Dein dir treie froy,

Perl Gilbo

67. PINCHAS TO PERL

My dear wife,

"Need breaks iron asunder." I have become a *melamed*. Do not imagine that it is easy work, it's a real slog. But it may be just in my case, being as I have just "one" boss and not being a teacher by nature. If I am not, I guess I will never figure out how human health can cope with teaching twenty to thirty children like the *melameds* do.

I hope they will definitely be happy with me and vice versa also. But I will never be happy with the work.

I am enclosing some money for you. I had it as an advance on the first month. Write and tell me if they accept a *melamed*'s money, too.

Your husband,

Pinchas Gilbo

Mein teiere froy!

"Noyt—brecht eizen." Ich bin a melamed gevoren, meyn nit az es iz a leichter arbet, es iz take an arbet. Nor es ken zein az nor bei mir, veil ich bin bei "eyn" balabos, veil ich bin nit keyn geborener melamed. Ven nit ken ich take nit klug veren vi halt es oys a mentshisher gezunt tsu lernen mit 20–30 kinder vi di melamdim tun.

Ich hof az zey velen fun mir gevis tsufriden zein, ich fun zey—oych; nor fun di arbet—vel ich keyn mol nit tsufriden zein.

Ich shik dir do gelt, ich hob es genumen far dem ershten monat faroys. Shreib mir oyb melamdishe gelt nemt men oych.

Dein man,

Pinches Gilbo

68. CHAIM TO NECHOME

Dearest Nechome,

What is the reason that I have not had a letter from you here for so long? Don't you know that I'm very concerned about it? I do not know what I should be worrying about, something must be happening there, so write me straight away about how you are keeping and about our dear little children. I want them to sign the letter in their own hand, my patience is utterly exhausted.

Your concerned husband,

Chaim Grossmann

Teierste Nechome!

Vos iz di urzache vos ich hob fun dir do lang keyn briv? Veystu den nit az ich bin fun dem zeyer umruhik? Ich veys nit vos ibertsutrachten, epes muz dortn zein, alzo shreib mir gleich fun dein gezunt un fun undzere libe kinderlech. Zey zolen eygenhendik dem briv untershreiben, ich hob shoyn mer keyn geduld nit!

Dein umruhiker man,

Cheiyim Grossmann

69. NECHOME TO CHAIM

My good Chaim,

I have received your letter. You are surprised that I have not written to you for so long. You are very concerned by it and do not know what to make of it. So I am writing to you that I and our two little children are, thank God, well. Everything at home is just fine. But the children should not allow me to write—I'm busy with them for days on end, and at night when I put them to bed I'm very tired and also fall asleep. That is the only reason that I do not often write to you.

Your wife,

Esther Grossmann

Mein guter Cheiyim!

Dein briv hob ich erhalten. Du vunderst zich vos ich hob dir do lang nit geshriben, du bizt derfun zeyer umruhik un veyst nit vos ibertsukleren. Alzo shreib ich dir dos ich un oych undzere tsvey kinderlech zenen danken got gezunt. In hoyz iz ales in besten ordnung. Nor di kinderlech zolen leben lozen nit shreiben—ich bin mit zey basheftikt gantse teg, un bei nacht az ich leyg zey shlofen bin ich zeyer mit un fal oych shlofen. Dos iz di eyntsike urzache fun mein nit oft shreiben tsu dir.

Dein froy,

Ester Grossmann

70. A WIFE TO A HUSBAND

My dear, beloved husband,

I am already intending to leave for home, the *dacha* season is already over. The doctors tell me that I am now, thank God, fully recovered—the spa has done a great deal for me. And so, my dear husband, send me some money, as I owe quite a lot here. The money I received from you not so long ago did not cover half my debts. I had to repay over fifty rubles to the dressmaker alone, twenty rubles to the milliner, and other such necessary expenses.

Send me the money as quickly as you can. I want to come home already.

Your wife,

Esther Dreyzel Peltzenstein

Teierer liber man!

Ich kloyb zich shoyn aheym tsu foren, der datse sezon hot zich shoyn geendikt. Di ertste zogen mir az ich bin yetst danken Got fulkum gezund—di bod hot mir zeyer farbesert. Alzo, mein teierer man, shik mir tsu gelt, vorem ich bin do fil shuldik. Di gelt vos ich hob fun dir nit lang erhalten hot nit fardekt a helft fun meine shulden. Ich hob nor di shneiderin aleyn opgetsolt iber fuftsik rubel, di putsmacherin tsvantsik rubel un noch a zelche neytike oysgaben.
Shik mir vos gicher dos gelt. Ich vil shoyn aheym kumen.

Dein froy,

Ester Dreyzel Peltsenshtein

71. REPLY

Dearest wife,

I may now call you "dear"- you are costing me "dear"[35] enough this summer. How does a person spend so much money on such bits of clothing which are simply unnecessary, for a few months in a vacation home? I would advise you to leave behind the "dear" items in Druzgenik, because where will you put them?

Your essential debts will have to be paid. I am sending you herewith _____ rubles and do what you wish with them, but just come on home, will you?

Your husband,

Elozor Peltzenstein

Teierste froy!

Ich meg dir itster rufen "teiere," du kost mir dem zumer genug "teier." Vi git men dos oys azoy fil gelt oyf a zelche shmates vos zeinen nor "iberik" oyf a por datse monaten? Ich volt dir raten du zolst di "teiere" chafeytsem in druzgenik iberlozen, vorem vu vestu zey ahinton?

---

35. The Yiddish play on the word *teier* translates into British English, where "dear" also means "expensive," but not into American.

Deine neytike choyves muz men batsolen. Ich shik dir do _____ rubel un tu mit zey vos du vilst, nor kum shoyn amol aheym.

Dein man,

Elozor Peltsenshtein

72. A WIFE TO A HUSBAND

Dearest Michael,

The season is coming to an end, everyone is traveling back home, and I must also leave. But I am writing to say that, frankly, I have no desire whatsoever to do so. You would not recognize me, so well am I recovered. What a thing not to run a house, not to bear any blame, and to live so well! This place is a real paradise. I have had very nice company here, particularly a neighbor of mine, a nice young German, never in my life have I met such a person. He left today already. Send me as much money as you can.

Your wife,

Lisa Kalmensohn

Teierster Michoel!

Der sezon endikt zich, ale foren aheym un ich muz oych foren. Ober ich shreib dir ofen az es vilt zich gor fun danen nit foren. Du volst mir yetst nit derkenen, aza gut hob ich zich derhoylt. A kleynikeyt nit firen keyn hoyz, nit hoben oyf zich keyn zind un leben azoy gut! Do iz an emeser gan-eyden. Ich hob do gehat zeyer gute gezelshaft; iber hoypt mein a nachbar, a sheyner yunger man a deitsh, ich hob noch in mein leben aza perzon nit getrofen. Er iz shoyn heint opgeforen. Shik mir gelt vos mer.

Dein froy,

Liza Kalmenson

Letters to Friends

73. TO A WOMAN FRIEND

Dear Clara,

When I was in Europe, you were my best friend, whom I told everything to in detail, and now that I am in America you are also the only one to whom I have to write out the details of everything that happens to me.

In this letter I am letting you know some important news: I am very happily engaged to be married! My fiancé is handsome, wealthy, and kind. Here, one does not go by education—one has to be a *mentsh*,[36] capable in business and in running a household, and he is absolutely all of that.

We met one another at a wedding, he liked me and—like an American, without playing games—he asked for my hand and that was that. He only asked for my hand, but I also gave him my heart. . . .

Your friend,

Tanya Rosenblatt

---

36. A decent person.

Beste Klara!

Als ich bin in Eyrope geven bistu mein beste freindin geven, far velche ich hob ales oys dertsoylt, un yetst uz ich bin in Amerike bistu oych di eyntsike far velche ich muz ales vos bei mir kumt for oysshreiben.

In dizen briv teyl ich dir mit a vichtike neies: Ich bin farlobt zeyer gliklech! Mein broytigam iz a sheyner, a reicher un a guter mentsh. Af bildung kukt men do nit—men darf a mentsh zein, feyik zein tsu gesheft un tsu firn a hoyz, un dos ales iz er fulkum.

Mir hoben zich af a chasene derkent, ich bin im gefelen gevoren un er—vi an amerikaner, on kuntsen—hot mein hand gebeten un avek arum. Er hot gebeten nor mein hand, ober ich hob im oych mein harts gegeben. . . .

Dein freindin,

Tanya Rozenblat

74. REPLY

Dear Tanya,

Congratulations! I wish you enduring happiness with the man whom you have made happy with your hand. America is a happy place, after all. You have been there for a total of five months and you have already made such a happy match.

I immediately announced the joyful news to everyone. They all wish you happiness and bliss, together with your beloved.

Write me when your wedding will be, God willing: I never imagined that I would not be at your wedding. But a person cannot calculate these things. Off you've gone to America and you are turning into an American lady.

Give my regards to your fiancé. I ask of him to love and cherish you always, as you so justly deserve.

Your friend,

Clara Sprinzon

Libste Tanya!

Ich gratulire dir! Ich vinsh dir eybik gliklech tsu zein mit dem vos du host mit dein hand baglikt. Amerika iz fort a gliklecher ort! Du bist dorten in gantsen finf monaten un host shoyn aza glikleche partiye geton.

Ich hob gleich alemen ongezogt di freyleche neies, ale vinshen dir glik un zegen mit dein hartsens gelibten tsuzamen.

Shreib mir ven vet mit glik eier hochtseit zein: Ich hob mir nimals forgeshtelt az ich zol af dein hochtseit nit zein. A mentsh ken ober nit oysrechnen: ot bistu in Amerika avek un du verst an amerikanka.

Gris dein liben broytigam in mein nomen: Ich bet im er zol dir imer liben un shetsen vi du bist vert.

Dein freindin,

Klare Shprintson

75. TANYA TO CLARA

My dear Clara,

I have conveyed your good wishes to my Jacob. He has also seen your photograph at my place. He says that if you should come to America, you would also find a good match, and I also think so. After all, you have a brother and a brother-in-law here. Make the trip—now at the beginning of summer is the best time for it.

Come without fail! I have a good future brother-in-law. He will like you and you will like him, too. I will be a matchmaker myself. Come, my dear, come and we will only see good things come to each other.

Yours affectionately,

Tanya

Libe gute Klare!

Ich hob mein Yakob'n dein grus ibergegeben, er hot oych bei mir dein fotografye (bild) gezen, er zogt az ven du zolst in Amerika kumen, volstu oych a gute partye geton, ich meyn oych azoy, do host doch do a bruder un a shvoger, mach dein reize—yetst, der onfang fun zumer iz dertsu di beste tseit.

Kum, nit andersh! Ich hob a gutn tsukunftiken shvoger, du vest im gefelen un er dir oych. A shadchente vel ich aleyn zein. Kum, meine teiere, kum un mir velen zen eyne af di tsveyte nor guts.

Deine dich shetsende,

Tanya

76. TO A WOMAN FRIEND

My dear Sophia,

You gave me great pleasure by writing that my letters always give you pleasure. One heart feels another. For me, it is quite simply a holiday when I receive a letter from you, and when I write you a letter, too. It seems to me that you have no other friend as devoted to you as I am. So I hope and pray that our letters never stop.

Your friend,

Rachel Gutkind

Libe beste Sofia!

Du host mir fil fargenigen farshaft mit dem vos du shreibst az meine briv farshafen dir imer fargenigen. A harts filt a harts—bei mir iz prost a yontef der tog in velchen ich derhalt fun dir a briv, un oych ven ich shreib dir a briv. Mir ducht zich az aza ibergebene freindin vi ich bin dir hostu nit noch eyne: alzo iz mein vunsh dos undzere briv zolen nimals oyfheren.

Dein freindin,

Rochl Gutkind

77. TO A MALE FRIEND

Dear friend,

Before I left, I promised to write you frequent letters, but I have not kept my word. I have been here eight weeks and have so far only written you a small letter about my arrival in Africa. You must already have assumed that I have become a perfect Englishman and have no shame about lying, but it is not like that! The reason I have not written is because I could not write or did not have what to write. The bottom line is that in Africa there is no gold in the streets either; by the time you get to Africa, your stomach gets all shaken out, but scarcely have you got to a place when your stomach shows that it's there. It disregards the fact that Africa is the land of gold and it just wants its dues. . . . It—the stomach—is a mean litigant; it will not wait until tomorrow, you cannot fob it off with words.

Now there are some signs of hope. When I have settled down, please God, I will write to you frequently. Write about yourself.

Your friend,

Aaron Tennenbaum

Yedid yokor venechmod!

Far mein opreizen hob ich dir farshprochn ofte briv tsu shreiben, nor ich hob nit gehaltn vort: es iz shoyn acht vochn vi ich bin do un hob dir noch ersht eyn kleynem briv vegen mein onkumen noch Afrika geshriben. Du host shoyn gevis gemeynt az ich bin gevoren a polener englender un shem zich nit mit a ligen, es iz ober nit azoy! Ich hob dir nit geshriben veil ich hob nit gekont shreiben oder nit gehat vos tsu shreiben. Di untershte shure iz az—in Afrika ligt oych keyn gold nit af di gasen, biz men kumt in Afrika treyslt zich zogar oys der mogen, ober koym kumt men shoyn af an ort veizt der mogen az er iz do. Er kukt gor nit vos Afrika iz di gold-land un er vil poshet zeins. . . . Er—der mogen—iz a shlechter moner, er vart nit af morgen, im ken men nit mesalek zein mit verter.

Yetst nemt zich mir etvos a hofnung veizen. Az ich vel im yirtse hashem zich bazetsen vel ich dir oft shreiben. Shreib fun zich.

Yedidcho,

Aren Tenenboym

78. REPLY

My dear friend Aaron,

I must write to tell you that I never began to doubt your word, and I believe that there are also real, decent people in England. I fully understood that in the first stages before you sort yourself out, there is nothing to write about and no time to write. Thank the Lord that there are some hopeful signs. Blessed is the country where there is room at least for hope! Please God, may you be happy in Africa.

About myself, what should I write to you? I toil like a mule and I get the same plagues as Pharaoh got. . . . Just you make yourself a living there and we will correspond, maybe I will also go to Africa.

Your friend,

Mordechai Gamse

Teierster freind Aren!

Ich muz dir shreiben az ich hob gor nit ongefangen tsveyflen in dein vort, un ich gloyb az in England iz oych do emese mentshen. Ich hob farshtanen az di ershte tseit befor men ordent zich ein iz nito vos tsu shreiben un ven tsu shreiben. Danken dem eybiken vos dir veizt zich a hofnung. Gebensht iz di land vu men ken chotsh hofen! Gibe Got du zolst tsufriden zein in Afrika.

Fun zich vos zol ich dir shreiben? Ich horeve vi an eyzel un hob vos Pare hot gehat. . . . Mach du nor dorten a leben, velen mir zich durchshreiben, fileicht vel ich oych geyn in Afrika.

Dein freind,

Mordche Gamze

79. TO A MALE FRIEND

My dear friend Raphael,

How are you, dear friend? It has been a long long time since we were in touch! But, as I remember, you remained in debt to me—you owe me a reply. But when it comes to writing, you are a bad payer, so I am showing you that good friends do not care about anything, and I am giving you something from the new account—*I* am writing.

How are you living, how are things going, and what are you doing with yourself? I am very keen to know all about it.

In two to three months' time my elder daughter is to be married, God willing, so I will enliven you a little, dear friend, and arouse you from your sleep. You will, as you can imagine, be the first and foremost of my guests.

Your friend,

Michael Bernstein

Mein bester freind Refoel!

Vos machstu, liber freind? Shoyn lang, lang hoben mir zich nit durchgeshriben! Nor vi ich gedenk bistu mir a bal choyv gebliben—du bist mir shuldik an entfer. Du bist ober in shreiben a shlechter tsoler, alzo veiz ich dir az gute freind kuken af keyn zach nit un ich gib dir fun dos neie akonte—ich shreib.

Vi lebstu, vi geyt dir un mit vos basheftikst du zich? Ich bin zeyer gern dos ales tsu visen.

In farloyf fun tsvey-drei chadoshim darf bei mein eltere tochter mit mazel chasene zein, alzo vel ich dir, liber freind, dermunteren a bisl un oyfveken fun dein shlof. Du vest doch bei mir der bester un ershter gast zein.

Dein freind,

Michoel Bernshtein

80. REPLY

My dear friend Michael,

Today, as we were all sitting and having tea at my house, we were just speaking about you. What can the reason be—my wife asked—that Bernstein has stopped writing? Is he angry with us or has he forgotten us? To be truthful, I had no answer to give her, but the mailman rescued me from embarassment—he handed me your letter, on which I said a *Shecheyonu* blessing.[37]

We are all well, thank God, we cannot complain about the living we make, and that is how we are living our life here in the small town. It usually comes nowhere near the living you make in New York, but we countryfolk are satisfied with what we have.

I will be coming to your daughter's wedding, please God, with my wife. She says that you deserve it.

Regards from all my children to your whole family.

Your friend,

Raphael Rabinovitch

---

37. According to religious custom, this blessing is said upon seeing a bosom friend after a month's separation.

Yedidi hayokor Michoel!

Heint als mir zeinen ale bei mir in hoyz bei tey gezesen, hoben mir grade vegen dir geret. Vos ken dos zein—hot mein froy gefregt—vos Bernshtein hot oyfgehert tsu shreiben? Iz er beyz af undz oder er hot undz fargesen? Ich hob ir af di varheit keyn entfer nit gehat tsu geben, nor der brivntreger hot mir fun farlegenheit bafreit—er hot mir dein briv derlangt af velchen ich hob shecheyonu gemacht.

Mir zeinen ale danken Got gezunt, parnose nit tsu farzindiken hoben mir, un azoy leben mir zich do in di kleyne shtetl. Gevoytnlech kumt es nit tsu dein leben in Nyu York, nor mir kontri-leit banugenen zich mit dos vos mir hoben.

Af dein tochters chasene im yirtse hashem vel ich kumen mit mein froy. Zi zogt az du bist dos vert.

Ale meine kinder grisen dein gantse familye.

Dein,

Refoel Rabinovitsh

81. MICHAEL TO RAPHAEL

My dear friend Raphael,

Things are pretty good and I am happy! Our old friendship has been on hold up to now; now we have given it an airing and it will be fresh again.

My family has had no end of pleasure to hear that you are all keeping well and making a living. My daughter, who is getting married, says that she deserves a thank-you—if she had not wanted her future husband, she would not be a bride-to-be, and if she were not a bride-to-be, I would not have invited you to a wedding and would perhaps not yet have made up my mind to write to you. But her future husband says that it is he who deserves the thank-you. But I told them that one should thank your good wife who is getting herself ready for going to the wedding, so we all wish to thank her.

You write that your life in the country does not come up to my life in New York. There is nothing one has less need of than to live in a great city. You do not live like you would want, everything seems to have been made by machine, including the running of a household. . . . No, my dear friend, there is nothing to be envious of.

Your friend,

Michael Bernstein

Bester freind Refoel!

Gants gut ich bin tsufriden! Undzer alte freindshaft iz zich oysgelegen biz a tsett. Yetst hoben mir ir oysgeluftert, un zi vet vider frish zein.
Mein familye zeinen unendlech tsufriden fun dein miteylung dos ir zeit ale gezunt un hot parnose. Mein tochter di kale zogt az ir kumt a dank—ven zi volt dem chosen nit velen, volt zi keyn kale nit zein, un ven zi volt keyn kale nit zein volt ich dir af chasene nit gebetn, un volt fileicht noch nit tsukleyben zich tsu shreiben tsu dir. Der chosen ober zogt az der dank kumt im, ich hob zey ober gezogt az der dank kumt dein gute froy velche ruft zich oys af chasene tsu kumen, alzo danken mir ir ale.
Du shreibst az dein leben in kontri kumt nit tsu mein leben in Nyu-York, men darf nit erger vi voynen in a groyse shtot: Men lebt nit vi men vil, es iz ales vi mit a mashin gemacht, zogar di firung in hoyz. . . . Neyn, liber freind, nito vos mekane tsu zein.

Dein freind,

Michoel Bernshtein

82. TO A MALE FRIEND

Dear Friend,

In my present predicament I have no one and nowhere to turn to but you. You did me many a good turn once upon a time, in good times, when things were well with me and I had lots of friends. So I fancy that you will not refuse me now either, now when your friendship with me can brighten my gloomy situation.

I will not give you a lecture. Short and sharp: I am destitute! All my business ventures have left me without a cent. . . . I am no more than a couple of people, but two people also have to eat as long as they are alive.

Believe me, worthy friend, when I tell you that no one at my end knows the bitter truth for the time being. I have revealed it to you alone.

Your unfortunate friend,

Benjamin Shershevsky

Bester freind!

In mein yetstike shlechte lage hob ich zich nit tsu vemen un vu tsu venden oyser tsu dir. Du host mir a mol in di gute yoren fil toyves geton, dan als mir iz gut geven un ich hob fil freind gehat. Du, alzo, rechen ich, vest mir yetst oych nit opzogen, yetst—ven dein freindshaft tsu mir ken mein finstere lage derleichten.

Ich vel dir fil nit onreden, kurts un sharf: ich bin an oreman! Fun meine ale gesheften hot zich oysgelozen dos ich bin on a sent gebliben. . . . ich bin zogar nor a por folk, ober tsvey mentshn darfen oych esen kol zman zey leben.

Gloyb mir, vertester freind, az dem biteren emes veys noch bei mir derveile keyner nit, ich hob dos nor dir antdekt.

Dein ungliklecher freind,

Binyomin Shershevski

83. REPLY

Ostrov, 18 April 1903

My dear friend Benjamin,

I am beside myself with your letter; it hit me like a bullet! Can you, my good friend, be so unfortunate? You are having to talk about being supported with your wife? Oh, what do my ears hear!

But moaning never filled a stomach. . . . I am sending you two hundred dollars. When God sends you help, you will mail it to me; and if your money runs out, I will lend you more, do not feel embarrassed—no one shall know of it but me.

Your friend,

Bunim

Teierster freind Binyomin!

Ich bin oyser zich fun dein briv, er hot mir vi a koyl getrofen! Du, mein bester freind, bist azoy ungliklech? Du darfst reden vegen unterhalten dem leben fun dir mit dein froy? Ah, vos meine oyern heren!

Nor mit kines iz men nit zat. . . . Ich shik dir tsvey hundert dolar, az Got vel dir helfen vestu mir zey opshiken; un az di gelt vet bei dir oysgeyn vel ich dir noch leien, shem zich nit far mir—oyser mir vet es keyner nit visen.

Dein freind,

Bunem

84. BENJAMIN TO BUNEM

Lyutsin, 25 April 1903

My dear friend,

You have infused us—myself and my downtrodden wife—with a new soul. Now I understand how true the proverb is, "You can spot a good friend when times are bad." Now, when I had no one to turn to, when I had it so bad, you lit up my dark night like the sun. May God grant that you with your dear children never know misfortune as long as you live.

I have ended up having to sell my home, because what use is it in the small town? I will charge a few hundred roubles for it and, with the money, I will depart for somewhere else where I am not known—there, I will open a small business and earn a living. What do you advise? Write to me.

Your friend,

Benjamin Shershevski

Mein teierer freind!

Du host undz, dos heyst mir un mein nidergeshlogener froy, a neshome areingezetst. Yetst farshtey ich vi richtik es iz der shprichvort: "A guten freind derkent men in a shlechte tseit." Yetst az ich hob nit gehat tsu vemen tsu venden zich, az mir iz gekumen gants shlecht, hostu mir vi di zun di finstere nacht erloychtn. Got zol dir helfen, du un deine libe kinder zolt tseit eier leben fun keyn shlechts nit visen.

Bei mir iz gebliben ich zol mein hoyz farkoyfen, vorem tsu vos ken zi mir nutsen in di kleyne shtetl? Ich vel far ir nemen etleche hundert rubel, un vel mit di gelt aroysforen andersh vu, vu men ken mir nit—dorten vel ich a kleyn gesheftl efenen un vel machen a leben. Vi iz dein eytse? Shreib.

Dein freind,

Binyomin Shershevski

85. BUNEM TO BENJAMIN

Ostrov, 2 March 1903

My dear friend,

I like your plan. In Lyutsin[38] everyone knows you as a homeowner who has fallen on hard times; that is not to be envied! But there in a strange town you will be opening a new chapter for yourself, another business, and God will help you. What can your house give you in the bleak, small town of Lyutsin? Better a rich lodger than a poor homeowner.

Your friend,

Bunem

Mein bester freind!

Dein plan gefelt mir. In Lutsen kenen dir ale far a gefalenem balabos, dos iz nit mekane tsu zein! Dorten ober in a fremde shtot vestu zich efenen noch dein kapitl noch a gesheft, un Got vet dir helfen. Vos ken dir geben dein hoyz in der vister shtetl Lutsin? Beser a reicher shochen eyder an oremer balabos.

Dein freind,

Bunem

---

38. Lyutsin is in today's Latvia, as are several other locations mentioned in the letters, such as Tukkum, Mitava, and Libava. In the 1905 edition, Lyutsin has been changed to Altona.

86. BENJAMIN TO BUNEM

Korsovka, 10 March 1903

Dear friend,

Your advice is just as a friend would give. I have left Lyutsin for Korsovka, to date a village where Jews were not allowed to live, meaning to settle. But it has now turned into a small township, our fellow Jews have moved in from many cities, where they live, poor wretches, packed together like herrings in a barrel—it has become a fine little town. I have already hit upon a business: I want to open a bookstore. I have submitted a petition to the governor to be allowed to do so, and I hope I will get it. My house fetched eight hundred rubles, so I am mailing you your two hundred rubles with thanks. Should the business require any more money, I will take a loan from you.

Your friend,

Benjamin Shershevski

Teierer freind!

Dein rat iz vi fun a freind. Ich bin aroys fun Lutsen in Korsovka; dos iz geven a dorf biz yetst, vu a yid hot nit getort voynen, dos heyst bazetsen zich. Yetst iz es ober gevoren a kleyn shtetel, es zenen ongeforen acheynu bney yisroel fun fil shtet, vu zey ligen nebech farpakt vi hering in a tun—es iz gevoren a feine shtetel. Ich hob zich shoyn oysgezen a gesheft: ich vil efenen a buchhandlung. Ich hob derlangt a bitshrift tsu dem gubernator, er zol mir dos erloyben; un hof az ich vel dos bakumen. Far mein hoyz hob ich genumen 800 rubel, alzo shik ich dir op mit dank deine 200 rubel. Oyb tsum gesheft vet zich foderen noch gelt, vel ich dan bei dir leien.

Dein freind,

Binyomin Shershevski

Making a Match

87. TO A MATCHMAKER

Shklov, 1 April 1903

Dear Mr. Menachem Arzelkovski,

Seeing as I have a fine daughter, blessed with personality and discrimination, with whom I am prepared to give five hundred rubles in cash, as well as two years' room and board, I am asking you to propose a good match. You know me well and I know one can rely upon you—since you are a man of means and a matchmaker.

Your friend,

Yitzchok Feinberg

Yedidi Reb Menachem Arzelkovski,

Azoy vi ich hob a gerotene tochter, a parshoyn un a kenerke, velche ich bin greyt tsu geben 500 rubel in mezumen oykh tsvey yor kest, bet ich eich mir a guten shidech fortsulegen. Ir kent mir gut un ich veys az oyf eich ken men zich farlozen—ir zeit doch a balabos a shadchen.

Eier freind,

Yitschok Feinberg

88. REPLY

Agatchov, 5 April 1903

Dear Reb Yitzchok,

If everything you write is correct (because your letter is dated April 1), I have a nice son-in-law for you. A good-looking young man from a fine family—a *melamed*'s[39] son; not a common sort of person, no physical defects, Heaven forbid, and what's more, someone who can bring in money, what we like to call a "breadwinner." Write to tell me the name of the bride.

Cordially,

Menachem son of Rabbi Arzelkovski

Yedidi Reb Yitschok!

Oyb es iz ales richtik vi ir shreibt (vorem eier briv iz geshriben 1 April), hob ich far eich a guten chosen. A sheyner bocher fun a feine familye—a melamed's a zun; nit keyn proster, nit keyn bal-mum chas vesholem, un dertsu a fardiner, vos bei undz ruft zich a "broyt-geber." Shreibt mir vi men ruft di kale.

Yedido,

Menachem ben ha-Rov Arzelkovski

---

39. See note 1.

89. A MATCHMAKER TO AN IN-LAW

Vilna, 8 May 1903

Dear, esteemed Reb Azriel,

Having heard from several people that you have an only daughter to whom you are giving a dowry of thirty to forty thousand rubles: the lady in question, as one says, is in no way exceptional, whether in looks or in education, but you are seeking to camouflage it with thousands— a fine veil, I daresay: with it you could even cover up a hunch. . . . I have had an idea for a match to propose to you. Just write to say whether it is true that you are also only after money. Also inform me in advance whether you will be paying me my travel expenses. Then I will come down to you to have a talk and, while we are at it, see the lady in question.

Yours respectfully,

Eliezer Sandomirski

Kvoyd Hagoen Reb Azriel,

Azoy vi ich hob gehert fun eynike mentshen az ir hot a bas yechido, velche ir git 30–40 toyzend rubel naden: di meduberes, vi men zogt, iz zogar nit keyn oysname, nit in sheynkeyt un nit in bildung, nor ir vilt dos fardeken mit toyzender—dos iz, muz ich eich zogen, a guter dek-tuch: men ken dermit fardeken a heyker oych. . . . Iz mir eingefalen eich a shidech fortsuleygen.

Shreibt mir nor oyb es iz emes az ir zucht oych nor gelt. Oych zeit mir moydia foroys oyb ir vet mir umkeren reize kosten. Vel ich tsu eich aropforen durchreden un zen agav di meduberes.

Mit eren gefile,

Eliezer Sandomirski

90. REPLY

Volkoviski, 12 May 1903

Dear Reb Eliezer, the Matchmaker,

I have not replied to you until today because my bookkeeper was not home, and I am not (I would not wish it on you) a very capable writer. A matchmaker, of course, must be told the truth. I am giving my daughter thirty to thirty-five thousand rubles but the young man must also have no less than twenty thousand and must come from a large city. My daughter, you understand, has been raised in a small town and so I want her to develop at least when she leaves my home. I am giving money and asking for money. I will pay your expenses upon betrothal. Before that, not one cent.

Cordially,

Azriel Schweinmann

Kvoyd Hashadchen Reb Eliezer

Ich hob eich biz heint nit geentfert veil mein buchhalter iz nit geven tsu hoyze. Un ich bin, loy aleychem, nit keyn groyser berye oyf shreiben. Far a shadchen muz men doch dem emes zogen. Mein tochter gib ich 30–35 toyzend rubel nor der yunger man zol oych hoben nit veyniker vi 20 toyzend, un zol zein fun a groyser shtot. Mein tochter, farshteyt ir, iz in a kleyn shtetel ertsaygen, alzo vil ich zi zol zich lechol hapoches antviklen az zi vet fun mir aroys. Ich gib gelt un foder gelt. Hoytsoes vel ich eich umkeren tsu tnoim. Frier—a groshn oych nit.

Yedidoy,

Azriel Shveinman

91. TO A MATCHMAKER

Bialistok, 10 June 1903

Dear Reb Meir, the Matchmaker,

There isn't a young person who can do without you, Reb Meir; if a matter is to be brought to a conclusion, you have to be there at the center of things. And why should you not earn something? After all, you aren't only doing it for the good deed's sake! Today I must also turn to you for help: "The evil inclination and a matchmaker are both unloved, and both obeyed," as the saying goes.

The matter is as follows: I love Mr. _____ 's daughter and she loves me, too. In other words, we are both in favor. But we have to see to it that our parents are also in favor; and this is where we need your assistance, Reb Meir. So be clear what you have to do. . . .

Here, right away, are ten rubles in cash for expenses. And for what the future holds, you can rest assured—the deal will reward you well.

Yosef Liebermann

Lehashadchen Reb Meyer!

On eich, Reb Meyer, ken keyn yinger mentsh zich nit bageyn, ir muzt in miten zein um a zach zol oysgefirt veren. Un far vos zolt ir take nit fardinen? Ir tut doch dos nit nor fun mitsve vegen! Ich muz oych heint tsu eich onkumen: "Dem yetser hore un a shadchen hot men nit holt, un men folgt zey," zogt zich a vertel.

Di zach iz azoy: Ich lib Reb _____ 's tochter; zi mir—oych, dos heyst mir velen beyde. Nor men darf doch ober zen az di elteren zolen oych velen; ot kumt men on tsu eich, Reb Meyer: alzo farshteyt vos ir hot tsu ton. . . .

Tsen kerblech hoytsoes hot ir do gleich mezumen, un oyf lehabo megt ir zicher zein—eich vet der eysek loynen.

Yoysef Liberman

92. REPLY

Grodno, second day of Sedra Tazria-Metzoyro

My dear, esteemed Joseph,

I am very happy that you have an appreciation of me. I hope that your appreciation will be still greater—Reb Meir knows how to get some work done. No sooner spoken than the deal's almost done. A letter of inquiry has already gone out, and I have already written about it to a partner of mine who is a matchmaker in Bialistok.

Yours truly,

Meir Axelrod

Lehabocher hamefursem Yoysef!

Mir freyt zeyer vos ir farshteyt mayn vert. Ich hof az ir vet es noch beser farshteyn—Reb Meyer ken oparbeten a shtikel arbet, geret un es iz korev lemeykech. Men hot shoyn geshikt onfreygen un ich hob shoyn vegen dem geshriben mein a shutef a byalistoker shadchen.

Yedidoy,

Reb Meyer Akselrod

Letters of Inquiry

93. CHAIM TO SHIMON

Grodno, 7 August 1903

Dear friend,

   A match has been proposed to me for my daughter with a son of _____ . So I am asking you, dear friend, if you could write to me fully and accurately about the family and the young man. I am relying on you because I know that you can be relied upon.

Your friend who awaits your reply,

Chaim Meizel

Yedid yokor!

Men leygt mir for a shidech far mein tochter mit _____ a zun. Alzo bet ich eich, bester freind, mir ales genoy vegen di familye un dem yungen man tsu shreiben. Ich farloz mich af eich veil ich veys az af eich ken ich zich farlozen.

Eier freind vos ervart eier antvort,

Cheiyem Meyzel

94. REPLY

Kirshanov, 13 August 1903

My dear friend Chaim Meizel,

On the matter of which you wrote to me, I have received some good information—good in all respects! You have to admit that a matchmaker can also sometimes have something reasonable to suggest. The thing looks very good to me. I advise you to ask another person as well. "One advisor is good, two are still better!"

Your friend,

Shimon Goldberg

Bester freind Reb Cheiyem Meyzel!

Ich hob vegen dem inyen vos ir hot mir geshriben gute oyskunfte bakumen—gut fun ale zeitn! Men muz moyde zein az a shadchen ken oych amol forleygen a gleiche zach, der inyen gefelt mir zeyer. Ich rot eich noch bei vemen oych tsu fregen, "eyn eytse iz gut, tsvey noch beser!"

Yedidcho,

Shimen Goldberg

95. IN ANOTHER MANNER

I am sorry, my friend, that you have come to me concerning information on the family _____ . I cannot give you a good opinion. I am not saying anything bad, as I have nothing of the sort to say.

Your friend, at your service,

John Doggone

Es tut leyd, mein freind, vos ir hot zich vegen oyskunfte iber di familye _____ . *Tsu mir gevendet. Ich ken eich keyn gute meynung nit geben. Keyn shlechts red ich nit, vorem ich hob nit vos.*

Eier freind, vos shteyt eich tsu dinst,

Dzshon Dogon

96. IN ANOTHER MANNER

The _____ family, regarding which you are asking me and going by my opinion, has written the same thing to me, too: they are inquiring of me about your son, about your household, and are going by me, also. So I am writing to you both in the same form of words: The whole thing looks very good to me, and I understand that it has been proposed by someone businesslike, not a windbag of a matchmaker. Please God, may it be brought to completion under a lucky star.

In heartfelt friendship,

David Werber

Di hoyz _____ af velchen ir fregt bei mir un farlozt zich af mein meynung hot mir oych dos zelbe geshriben: Zey fregen bei mir on af eier zun, af eier hoyz un farlozen zich oych af mir. Alzo shreib ich eich beyden dem zelbiken nusech: Mir gefelt di zach zeyer far pasend, un ich farshtey az dos hot forgeleygt a sochrisher mentsh, nit a ployderzak a shadchen. Gib Got dos zol mit mazel oysgefirt veren, in a gute sho.

Eier freind fun tifen hartsen,

Dovid Verber.

Letters of Invitation

97. TO A WEDDING

Kiev, 19 September 1903

Dear friend,

A time has come when you can show me how far your friendship with me extends, and how well you remember me—my elder son will be getting married, please God, in ten days (may it be for the best). So get ready to make the trip. The wedding will be in Minsk. When we are departing, I will wire you, and you will come by train and travel with us.

Your friend,

D. Shmudenisky

Bester Freind,

Es iz gekumen a tseit az du kenst mir veizen vi veit dein freindshaft tsu mir iz, un vi veit du gedenkst mir—bei mein eltern zun vet im yirtse hashem in tsen teg arum chasene zein mit mazel. Alzo mach zich reize fartik. Di chasene vet zein in Minsk, az mir velen aroysforen vel ich dir depeshiren, du vest af dem ban kumen un vest mit undz mitforen.

Dein freind,

D. Shmudenisky

98. REPLY

Homel, 22 September 1903

Dear Daniel,

I do not need much asking. I will certainly travel with you, please God, to the wedding and we will indeed have a great time. Wire me just one day beforehand which is the train by which you will be passing through, so that I can leave my business for a few days.

Your friend,

Abraham Shambadal

Teierer Doniel!

Du farshporst mir fil tsu beten, ich vel im yirtse hashem gevis mit eich foren af der chasene un mir velen take gut farbrengen. Depeshir mir nor mit a tog frier mit velchen tsug ir vet durchforen, ich zol kenen mein gesheft iberlozen af etleche teg.

Dein freind,

Avrom Shambadal

99. INVITATION TO AN ENGAGEMENT

Vitebsk, 5 April 1903

Dear friends,

Our dear daughter is getting engaged (may it be for the best). We are making a match after our own heart. The engagement will take place next Tuesday, so we are inviting you to honor us with your presence and to participate in our family celebration.

Your friends, who are ready and willing to do the same for you at any time,

Zalman and Sarah Schneersohn

Beste freind!

Undzer libe tochter vert mit mazel a kale, mir tuen a partye noch undzer vunsh. Dem kumendiken dinstik vet zein tnoim, alzo betn mir eich undz tsu baeren mit eier ersheinen tsu undz, un onteyl nemen in undzer hoyz yontef.

Eiere freind, velche zeinen bareit eich mit dos zelbe tsu dinen tsu yeder tseit.

Zalmen *un* Sore Shnerson

100. TO A *BRIS*

Polotsk, 10 June 1903

Dear friend,

God has favored me with a son; yesterday morning my dear wife gave birth to a son. You can imagine our joy. So I am inviting you to be sure to come to the circumcision.

Your friend,

Zalman Neuhaus

Bester freind!

Got hot mir mit a zun baglikt, gestern dos morgens hot mein libe froy mir a zun geboyren. Undzer freyd kenstu zich forshtelen. Alzo bet ich dir nit andersh tsum bris tsu kumen.

Dein freind,

Zalmen Neihoyz

Letter of Congratulation

101. LETTER TO A FRIEND

Dear friend,

I have received your engagement card. I have just one wish for you: May you and your worthy fiancée be granted all that you wish yourselves.

Your friend,

Boris Schattenstein

Bester freind!

Dein farlobungs-karte hob ich erhalten. Ich vinsh dir dos eyntsiks: es zol erfilt veren vos du un dein geerteste broyte vinsht zich zelbst.

Dein freind,

Boris Shatenshtein

Letter of Condolence

102. ON THE DEATH OF A FRIEND'S WIFE

Esteemed friend,

I only learned today of the misfortune that has befallen you, that you have lost your dear wife. Alas! Where shall I find sufficient words to express on paper what my heart feels?

I am with you in your grief! I can put myself wholly into your position, my sad friend. I feel your heavy pain. For who else knows as I do what a support you have lost?

But what help can one be? Against God's retribution no protest can avail. You have been grievously punished, nothing can be done, and you must now prove that you are a man of courage, a brave hero who can bear life's struggle with patience, for what can you gain from your despair, your weeping, and your lamentations?

Courage, my friend! As long as we live, we must never lose courage, your wife has now gone the way we all must go, and if God has deprived you of such a support, He will Himself surely guard and support you with His hand from this day on.

I believe that you are man enough to bear this blow. Be brave and take comfort.

Your friend,

Isaac Dov Eisenstein

Verter freind!

Ich hob ersht heite erforen fun dem umglik vos dich iz getrofen, dos du host deine libe gute froy farloyren. Ach! Vu nem ich do file vorten ich zol kenen af dem papir oysdriken dos vos mein harts filt?

Imcho onoychi betsoro! Ich gey gentslech arein in dein lage, mein ungliklecher freind. Ich fil deine groyse shvere shmertsen. Den ver veys noch vi ich vos far a shtits du host farloyren?

Ober vos ken men helfen? Gegen Gots shtrafe helft keyn protest, du bist hart bashtraft gevoren, es iz shoyn a farfalene zach, un du muzt yetst baveizen az du bist a man mit mut, a tapferer held vos ken geduldik ertrogen dem lebenskamf, den vos vet dir helfen dein fartsveyflung, dein veinen un dein klogen.

Mut, mein freind! Kol zman mir leben, darfen mir keyn mol dem mut nit farliren. Dein froy iz yetst gegangen in dem veg vuahin mir ale muzn geyn un ven Got hot fun dir aza shtitse tsugenemen, vet er gevis fun heint un veiter aleyn mit zein hand dich shitsen un shtitsen.

Ich gloyb az du bist man genug dizn shlog tsu ertrogen. Zei mutik un getreyst vi dir Vinsht dein freind,

Yitschok Dov Eizenshtein

Letters from Children

103. FROM A CHILD TO PARENTS

Dearest parents,

I arrived in G. an hour ago. All my uncle's children met me in the waiting hall. Tomorrow my uncle is going to send for the teacher and make an arrangement with him.

Your son,

Chaim Cohen

Gute libe eltern,

Ich bin ongekumen mit a sho tsurik in G. Dem onkels ale kinder hoben mir beim vachzal emfangen. Morgen vet der onkel (feter) shiken noch dem lerer un vet mit im opreden.

Eier zun,

Cheiem Kohen

104. TO A BROTHER

Dear brother,

My parents are writing you a letter, and I send a small hello. Thank you very much for not forgetting to ask after me in every letter. I already know how to study and write.

Your brother,

Tuvye Katzenellenbogen

Ach yokor,

Di eltern shreiben dir a briv un ich a kleynem grus. Ich dank dir zeyer, vos du fargest nit in yeder briv mir tsu grisen. Ich ken shoyn lernen un shreiben.

Dein bruder,

Tuvye Katzenellenbogen

105. TO A SISTER

Dear sister,

I also very much wanted to come with Mother to see you, but I just can't spare the time. I'm studying Hebrew, English, and arithmetic; next term I'll be through with *cheyder* and I'll be studying at home. Regards to your children.

Your brother,

Yisroel Feigelson

Libe shvester,

Ich hob oych zeyer gevolt mitforen mit di muter tsu dir, nor es iz shode di tseit. Ich lern hebreish, english un rechnung, dem kinftiken sizon (zman) vel ich shoyn aroys fun cheyder, ich vel lernen in der heym. Gris deine kinder.

Dein bruder,

Yisroel Feigelson

106. TO AN UNCLE

Dear Uncle,

I'm writing you a short hello in my father's letter. I can't write a lot as I have little time: I have to prepare lessons for three teachers—Gemara, Hebrew, and English.

Your nephew,

Yehuda Katzenellenbogen

Ledoydi hayokor,

In mein foters briv shreib ich eich a kleynem gris. Ich ken fil nit shreiben veil ich hob veynik tseit. Ich hob tsu machen lektsionen far drei lerers—Gemore, Hebreish un English.

Eier plimenik,

Yehuda Katzenellenbogen

107. TO A GRANDFATHER

To my dear grandfather,

I am sending you my wish for the New Year: May God give you good fortune, long years, and may you always have pleasure from your children. Please God that I should be able to write you such wishes many more times; this is the wish of your grandchild,

Leyb Garfinkel

Le'ovi zkeyni hayokor,

Ich shik eich mein vunsh tsum neiem yor: Got zol eich geben glik, lange yoren un ir zolt hoben imer fergnigen fun eiere kinder. Gib Got ich zol eich azelche vunsh briv fil mol shreiben, dos iz der ferlang fun eier eynikl,

Leyb Garfinkel

108. TO A GOOD FRIEND

My dear friend,

I would like you, my good friend, to share my pleasure, so I am writing to tell you that I have passed the examination. I received very good grades for everything. I am now already in third grade.

Your friend,

Michael Liliental

Yedidi hayokor,

Ich vil az du, mein guter freind, zolst mit mir mein fargenigen teylen, alzo shreib ich dir ontsuzogen az ich hob dem ekzamen gut oysgehaltn. Ich hob zeyer gute meinungen bakumen far ales. Ich bin shoyn yetst a shiler fun driter klas.

Yedidcho,

Michoel Liliental

109. REPLY

My good friend Michael,

I am very pleased that you did well in the examination. See to it that you go on studying hard, and you will always receive good grades. I am studying privately but very well.

Your friend,

Nachman Tannenbaum

Bester freind Michoel,

Mir freit zeyer vos du host gut oysgehalten dem ekzamen. Ze oych veiter fleisik tsu lernen, vestu ale mol gute meinungen bakumen. Ich lern privat, ober zeyer gut.

Dein freind,

Nachman Tannenbaum

110. A BOY TO HIS FRIEND

My friend Avrom,

I'm sure you'll need no asking, this evening, to my birthday at eight o'clock. The whole of our *cheyder* is going to be there. After all, we don't have to go to *cheyder* tomorrow, so today we can be up a bit later.

Your friend,

Yone Phillips

Tsu mein freind Avrom,

Loz zich nit beten heint ovend, acht a zeyger af mein geburtstog. Es vet keyner nit farfelen tsu kumen fun undzer cheyder, morgen velen mir doch in cheyder nit geyn, kenen mir heint abisel shpeter oyf zein.

Dein chaver,

Yoyne Filips

111. TO A FRIEND

Lend me a pen. I didn't realize at home, before I went to *cheyder*, that my pen's broken. I can't get away now from *cheyder* to buy one, or else the teacher will get mad at me. To show my gratitude, I'll give you a new pen tomorrow in return.

Your friend,

Gad Merlinski

Lei mir a feder. Ich hob zich nit arumgezen tsu hoyz, eyder ich bin in cheyder gegangen, az mein feder iz tsebrochen. Yetst fun cheyder ken ich nit geyn koyfen, der lerer zol nit beyz veren af mir. Morgen vel ich dir mit a dank opgeben a neie feder.

Dein freind,

Gad Merlinski

112. A PUPIL TO A TEACHER

My esteemed teacher,

I cannot come to *cheyder* today. My mother has given my shoes in to be repaired. So do not wait for me. Send my Bible, as well as my *Toldos Yisroel*,[40] with my little brother. I will review what I learned last week.

Your pupil,

Yaakov Dozin

Lemoyri hanichbod,

Ich ken heint in cheyder nit kumen. Di muter hot meine shich gegeben farrichten. Alzo zolt ir af mir nit varten. Shikt durch dem ingel mein tanach oych mein Toldes Yisroel. Ich vel viderholen (iberchazeren) vos ich hob di forike voch gelernt.

Eier talmid,

Yaakov Dozin

---

40. A Jewish history book.

About the Author

Lewis Glinert is a professor of Jewish language and culture at London University's School of Oriental and African Studies and chair of its Centre for Jewish Studies. Educated at Magdalen College, Oxford, where he was Doncaster Scholar of German, he has also held appointments at Haifa and Bar-Ilan universities and a visiting associate professorship at the University of Chicago. He is author of the definitive *The Grammar of Modern Hebrew* (1989), the best-selling *Joys of Hebrew* (1992) and *Hebrew in Ashkenaz: A Language in Exile* (1993), and has written and broadcast widely on Hebrew and Yiddish culture and linguistics, including two BBC documentaries, *Tongue of Tongues* and *Golem! The Making of a Modern Myth*. He lives in London with his wife, Joan, and their three children.